Rights and Disclaimer Statement

Please Note

All of the information provided in this text is based on the techniques and methods utilized by the author, and may not necessarily be applicable in your own situation. Please, before commiting yourself to *any* program of recovery, check with your physician first.

Table of Contents

Section One

Section One Wrap-Up

Section Two

Section Two Wrap-Up

Section Three

Section Three Wrap-Up

Section Four

Section Four Wrap-Up

Section Five

Section Five Wrap-Up

This book is dedicated first to my Mom and family, as they had apparently saw in me what I could not myself. Secondly, to Bob and Nancy. I just could not have done it without you guys. Lastly, to my nephew Hunter..."here come the Mercenaries."

Section One

The life of a heroin addict is tremendously eventful. The burden of securing funds to carry on as such, day in and day out, makes for a situation that simply does not allow for dull moments. Few have had less dull moments than myself, and while it *is* unfortunate, my friends, family, and the correctional system can all attest to this fact. I have known and crossed paths with countless others, of which very few have exhibited the drive and ambition to destroy themselves with which I had exuded for so long. I had made of self-destruction, an art, a science, and a mockery all at once. In retrospect I have but little understanding of what it was I was even chasing. There is no logic to be factored when an individual who had had a passion for life such as my own, yet was so seemingly determined to extinguish it.

I have been addicted to one thing or another for most of my life. For the last *two* decades I have been consumed by numerous fixations of all sort. Pills, marijuana, cocaine, amphetamines, nicotine, caffeine, television, candy, video games, you name it, I've probably abused it. However, it was my infatuation with the *opiate* that had given me that final shove over the edge and into the dark, menacing underworld of drug addiction.

Back some years ago there was a rather popular American journalist/writer named George Plimpton, you may or may not have heard of him. He was an immensely famous writer, who was famous most of all for his journalistic methods. You see, what Plimpton did was he would begin by selecting an athletic type of occupation, such as professional baseball player for example. He would then go on to spend several weeks and sometimes months training with an actual professional ball club, before finishing off by throwing out the first pitch and playing in a real major league baseball game. He did all of this as a unique form of rogue journalism, and so for each career he would take on, he would then report on the experience by writing a book about it. Plimpton had this rare ability to provide the 'common man' with an unparalleled birds-eye view into worlds that only a handful of others had *ever* seen.

The public had grown to adore and anticipate his books, and Plimpton went on to become a famously well known writer. George was one who enjoyed rubbing elbows with the elite. In fact, his best friends were the Kennedy's and they had spent loads of time together (he and Robert were classmates growing up). Plimpton had helped to found *The Paris Review*, which is a periodical that, while it was well read among the literary community, had typically been of somewhat modest *commercial* exposure otherwise. It is well known that George was often responsible for keeping the Review alive financially, by pumping in a steady flow of his own personal funds. However, in addition to George, the company had some other *interesting* donors that (more than likely) hadn't ever received any honorable mentions. It has been quoted on more than one occasion that the CIA was at one time a secret financier for the Review. It has also been widely rumored that Plimpton was some kind of affiliate to the CIA, using the magazine to encrypt secret communications as well as mask covert operations.

George *had* also been known to sometimes come off as a bit of a snob, even by his own children's accounts, but all in all he was considered by most as a genuinely likable fellow. I was intrigued with his persona and techniques and I found that I could make use of his methods as a way to enhance the effectiveness of my own writing.

I had elected to make the most productive use possible out of *my* twenty years experience, spent as an addict, inmate, and ex-con, by adapting it to my project here, in a (theoretically) similar fashion with which Plimpton would use the time *he* had spent, training and participating (in one instance) as a professional boxer. On account of the fact that I had always enjoyed writing, I would adapt my experience as a sort of journalistic investigation, and report the information in a creative comprehendable manner. This text has been designed in such a way that aims to place the reader firmly in the shoes of the subject. My focus throughout this work has been to grant the reader exclusive access to this harrowing world that manages to keep so many hostage, and, effectively enable them to experience the chaos and discord that *I* had gone through, in a way that will prepare them to accept the help offered here, or *anywhere*.

Have I found *all* the answers? Shit no. But, what I *have* found is a way out of this maze that so many are trapped in right this very minute, doomed to spend their days chasing their tails with no end in sight. What I have created could be thought of as a supplemental guide that just happens to unfold as I tell the tale of an addict among addicts.

My time on this earth has been riddled with tumultuous coincidence. As you will learn, I should have been dead numerous times over. I had brought myself to the brink of death many times only to be yanked back by the wonders of modern science (naltrexone), and had come to realize that my story had yet to even begin. There was much to be done, and above all, there was still one more chapter left regarding this business of addiction. One more chapter left to reveal to those in *our* world the rabbit hole that tunnels out of this disaster.

I have not included every detail regarding recovery, and I leave the responsibility of finding further information on you (should you require it). I have instead chosen to create a text that is geared toward those individuals who have been through the ringer, as I have, and should already be aptly informed of the basic lessons and methods aimed at helping one to attain sobriety. This is the stuff that hasn't been covered, and is laid out here in a way that does not follow the norm. The story that I present you with here *could* serve as an ideal companion for the addict who has not responded well to the treatments that are widely used, and is interested in perhaps seeking out another angle. This particular approach is one that focuses on the readers capacity to, not only rise above his addiction, but to rise above *all* struggles no matter what they are, and succeed in all facets of life.

When writing this book there *were* times I feared I may be chasing a dream, destined to become the 'Father McKensey' that Paul McCartney once spoke of. However, the way I've chosen to look at it is like this, if even *one* individual's life is affected in a positive light by my creating it, then I shall deem the book an absolute success.

Burt's Intro

Burt came into my life at what can only be described as the absolute perfect time. I was currently battling for my soul on a day to day basis, but just happened to be of the right frame of mind to accept help from an outside source, which was often not the case. What could I do? Nothing had worked so far and the drug runs were getting exhausting. Not to mention the whole experience had begun to take a serious toll on my physical well being.

The way in which Burt and I had met seemed completely random. Yet, as time went on I began noticing curious coincidences within this randomness. Eerily, I began to spot traits in Burt (who was this complete stranger to me) that would have within them faint traces of past relatives who had since passed on. For example, a turn of phrase that I hadn't heard since a certain family member was alive, or a facial expression that would look startlingly familiar. But that was Burt, he had this rare kind of mystique that was truly captivating. In all my time I had never met another person that was more full of surprises than he. Burt was on a quest just as I was, but it was the way in which our two paths had combined and what became of that *chance* meeting that still keeps me awake some nights, left with many questions.

Burt would often refer to himself as a student of the universe. He was noticeably intelligent and held many unique beliefs. He saw the world through an inquisitive eye and had learned long ago just how to apply new life lessons as they were learned. This, coupled with his ability to genuinely engage anyone (and adapt himself to their level), created in him a guru of sorts.

He was the kind of guy that would, even at his age (which was up there), give you one of those fake karate chops, you know, to make you flinch. Then, while talking to him he'd give this impression that there was just no question he couldn't answer, like Google. Not only was he usually *able* to form some kind of answer, but he was also willing. His brilliance would twinkle at the most random of times. For example, while attending a local fair over the summer, a car had pulled over with a young couple who needed directions to a hospital, only they did not speak a word of English and their mother was in the backseat screaming in some unfamiliar language (with what we later found out to be a bursting appendix). Burt was nearby and had caught wind of the situation. He quickly approached the vehicle and without hesitation broke into a rapid, fluent conversation in some rare dialect of Mandarin. He helped get the woman to the ER and perhaps may have even saved her life in the process.

It was when I had gotten locked up some years prior on a felony drug charge, that I began to take notice of the events leading up to and thereafter each incarceration. I then made a decision to do everything in my power to take advantage of any and all programming that the prison had to offer me by way of rehabilitation. Before long I had earned my G.E.D. and was soon attending various college courses (where I held a 4.0 GPA). I had also earned a stack of certifications for several occupational and relapse prevention/substance abuse education courses, and, though I did relapse at some point after my release, the drug runs *were* getting shorter each time. However, while they did get shorter, they had also become far more intense.

It wasn't long after my *final* sentence that Burt and I had met. He and I would go on to forge a solid connection over the next two years, and as a result, my life began to change in a way that I had yet to experience thus far. Burt shed light onto a world that I may have never been exposed to otherwise, and had helped me to harness the positivity within myself so that I may wield it wherever I choose. It seemed to happen overnight. Suddenly, with no training and even less *natural* ability, my attempts at the most mundane of things, such as drawing for instance, were finally yielding some actual quality artistic results. I was now able to make effective use of a pencil, producing images and portraits that I must admit had even taken myself by shock. There were other (similar) occurrences going on as well. After twenty years of meddling with the guitar (off and on), I had discovered that what at one time had been 'hidden' melodic scales, now began revealing themselves to me in small sporadic doses. Making use of this, my fingers began moving faster and more fluently.

Ever since I had been a child I felt as though I could manage to work my way through any assortment of tasks, with enough practice. Although, the situation here was of quite a different nature. It was as if I had been somehow awakened inside. Little by little my life began taking shape in a number of ways. My memory appeared to be improving, my body was beginning to feel healthier than ever before, and I was noticeably in a far better mood. The grass began to look greener to me, the sky more blue.

Burt was persistent in assuring me that these *new* feelings of mine, weren't new at all. He would often remind me that this was all a result of the fact that I had been caught up in addiction for so long, that I had eventually just lost sight of who I *thought* I was and wanted to be. He would then go on to say that I was now in the process of becoming one again with my true self and reestablishing who it is that I was and *am* deep down.

One other point which he had consistently made clear, was that I was not to squander this gift of clarity. To him it was paramount that I use this fresh new outlook on life to try and help those others who are still lost, find *their* way back to a safe and productive lifestyle.

It was a powerful motivating factor for me, the way in which Burt had stuck with me through thick and thin (mostly thin). Especially at a time when all possibilities of a real life had seemed, to me, utterly *im*possible. Anyone who knew me would certainly vouch that it was only a matter of time before I was, either (a) going to take an early dirt nap, or (b) catch a lengthy prison sentence. After my countless attempts at sobriety, a ten page criminal record, and a bout with depression (the likes of which most will *never* know), and still, just as my family had, Burt saw something in me that I could not see for myself. I feel that I owe a great bulk of my success thanks to his efforts (though he would tell me to give myself more credit).

The Stoned Philosopher

First and foremost, I must make clear to you that this text was not meant to be regarded as an instructional or educational tool. Yet instead it should be thought of simply as a story based on one man's unique approach to an altogether crippling affliction, that *could* perhaps help to guide an individual who is involved in an ostensibly unending battle for their own life with this gruesome killer. By no means do I suggest that you avoid any of the other programs or medicines that were designed (and are available) to aid you in your quest for tranquility.

My name is C. Alan Taylor, and I have personally participated in *almost* every form of rehabilitation available. I can say with confidence that given the right circumstances, anyone can very well achieve quality sobriety with most *any* program. The issue here being that 'the right circumstances,' are based on a multitude of factors, including but not limited to: proper support networks, degree of addiction, and state of mind (believe me, this list goes on and on). Unfortunately most addicts are not in circumstantially ideal scenarios, and what often occurs is another failed attempt results. Although some clean time *can* be achieved, our addictive behavior tends to lurk in the shadows ready to pounce on us when we least expect it. Complacency can often be a major hurdle for many addicts new to recovery. Fresh in sobriety, the addict will typically experience a unique form of amnesia, where as all the pain, discomfort, and misery somehow temporarily disappear from the memory, which I feel is the real genius this affliction wields over us.

So what happens next is the individual then relapses, only now with quite a bit more vigor than ever. Still, if they can manage to stay safe (and alive) until the next interruption in activity (there are always going to be spans of sober time, welcome or not), then there is a lesson learned and various 'tools' are acquired in the process. Now, I had mentioned 'tools,' which is a term heard often in recovery, and it refers to the advice and lessons one picks up along the way. At the peak of my own drug activity I was equipped with a *virtual* toolbox equivalent to that of a NASCAR mechanic, and still yet I was deeply entrenched in the addict lifestyle. As I had mentioned before, it is of the utmost importance that at least some of the right circumstances be in place.

It has been one of my objectives right from the start of this book, to show you that there *are* ways in which these circumstances can be modified (or manipulated) to suit the situation at hand. For instance, in Alcoholic Anonymous there is an unofficial slogan that states: "Fake it 'til you make it." Now let's say an addict is unwilling to even consider treatment and is in grave danger (an active addict is always in danger). In this situation, concerned family members can have the individual committed to a thirty day residential/lock down facility, where the patient would be obligated to attend programming as a means of 'earning' their way to a discharge. All of this is accomplished by having the family go and petition the court to have the individual arrested (with no legal implications), and transported to whichever facility falls under your particular jurisdiction, assuming your county has one (many do now).

However, not all states do offer this option and so you will have to check with your local district courthouse. I will tell you that I have seen this tool used many times and have also been witness to it saving a life or two. It is certainly something worth considering, should you find yourself in this kind of scenario.

While I wouldn't put much stock in this idea having a whole lot of success with a seasoned addict, perhaps parting an individual who is *early* in addiction away from their substance, could effectively deliver one swift, sharp dose of reality and shake their mind like a snow-globe, rearranging the individual's thought processes as the 'settling' occurs. If not, they can always just smile and nod their way through the program with the family's hope that the individual will see, hear, or feel *something* that manages to burrow through the walls of denial and guilt that have been hastily built by the disease (*fake it til they make it*). Just maybe there will be something that touches their soul in a way that begins to alter their perception of how they see themselves and the world around them. This does happen, although nowhere near as often as we would all appreciate.

It is my intent to assist you, the reader, in your search for answers to these and other questions surrounding this ever growing epidemic. This is a fascinating world we live in, one that continues to brim with secrets that science has yet to demystify. Who truly knows *what* the future holds. I have spent twenty plus years of *my* life seeking out a solution to this problem, and only when I took a step back did a solution find me. Is it fool proof? Absolutely not. But, it is assured that with immense effort and patience, each one of us has within us the will and the fortitude to stop this runaway train dead in it's tracks. That, I can promise is the absolute fact of the matter. We all deserve to live the life of our choosing, *if* we choose to pursue it.

In order for you to gain a proper understanding of *my* transformation and how exactly it came to be, you must first learn of the journey that took me to the edge of mortality and back again.

This is nasty business this double edged sword that we have come to know simply as, the opiate. In any form, opiates are powerful both in strength *and* influence. They can bring a king to his knees and a peasant to untold riches. They have been with us for thousands of years and will remain for many more. No matter what precautions are taken, they are sure to remain a thorn in our societies collective side, as well as the serum that will be used to treat the thorn's *puncture*.

The Opiate

Although archeologists *have* found evidence showing that the Mesopotamian and other ancient civilizations were cultivating the opium poppy as far back as 4000 years ago, it did not hit *our* shores until the 18th century, when the Chinese first began to show up on the west coast. These were people who were migrating to America with hopes of a new life, earning decent wages as laborers working on the (soon to be) coast to coast railroad track. Many of the immigrants brought with them connections from the old country to ship large quantities of black tar opium back into San Francisco Bay. Once they had established themselves and made the right connections, the shipments began floating in. And so it began in America, a fight that continues still today over 230 years later.

These immigrants began setting up opium dens where you could purchase the drug, and were allowed an area of space to sit, smoke, and relax. Many of these dens had bedrooms available, *as well as prostitutes*, and were a big draw for the sailors coming into San Francisco bay. In fact, the term 'shang-highed,' was used to describe the way in which shipmates would get a sailor high enough on opium (or liquor), that they were able to kidnap the man and force him to work as a crew member on a shipping vessel. Shipping captains were having a hard time getting new recruits, on account of the fact that pirates were ravaging the seas and killing many a ship hand, and so, they in turn often resorted to these and other seedy tactics.

By the time the drug truly took a foothold, one third of our country's population was plagued by some form of opiate addiction. This tells us that our ancestry has written the addiction process straight into our DNA, which could explain why, for some of us, this addiction needed no assistance in reeling us in. We were fully prepared to jump right in with both feet right from the start. When researching the topic, I had learned how an individuals genetic tendencies toward addiction are now being explained as a sort of side effect of other *known* genetic traits that have been passed on to the individual. The idea, is that these are negative traits which render the subject altered in such a way that could perhaps make for a more challenging existence when compared to the "average" individual. It is the result of living through life with this genetically passed mental health issue or physical abnormality (however minor) that researchers are now saying may be the link between genetics and addiction. Thankfully, Burt had taught me that there is no such thing as an addict who is unable to change his life. This means that, while you should know of these types of facts and how they can relate to you, do not allow them to weigh *too* heavily on your mind and in effect hinder your success.

Back *in* those early days, there were many more terminal diseases and severely painful ailments for which there weren't any effective treatments available. For this they had created morphine, and were then able to at least help those who needed it through the pain of dying. Many mothers also used this morphine, nightly, on themselves *and* their children. This was so, to the point that many children at this time were growing up comatosed, malnourished, and in overall poor health.

It was 1897 when a European pharmacist at Bayer Pharmaceutical, Felix Hoffman, attempting to synthesize codeine (which was to be less addictive than morphine), instead created something one and a half *times* the strength of morphine, and thus discovered the ability to synthesize heroin. His wife was severely ill and he wanted to bring her some kind of relief. He administered the drug to her hoping to provide her with a bit comfort, and after some time he began to increase the dose. She was having fair success with the drug until, through no intent of Felix's, the wife had overdosed and died. Hoffman went public with pleads to the people warning of the drug's lethal side effects, but it was too late. What had begun as an effort to relieve a painful cough was now taking the nation by storm.

Heroin would remain legal to possess and sell for some time, and soon the Sears and Roebuck catalog was offering its *own* kit. This kit included a vial, syringe, a couple of doses of Heroin, and a handy carrying case to tote it all around in for $1.50. Sir Francis Burton Harrison, an up and coming politician, found this all to be very alarming and began scouring the law books for an effective angle on curbing it.

It wasn't long after that, that doctors began experimenting with ways to deliver the drug to the body's system in a way that might lessen the chances of addiction. The answer *they* came up with, the hypodermic needle.

Imagine that. The idea was that they would bypass the stomach, where *they* believed the addiction process began. They would use this needle to deliver the drug to the system in a revolutionary manner. This allowed the medication to be introduced directly to the bloodstream, and, while proving quite useful ever since, the hypodermic needle would go on to turn the world of *opiate* addiction completely upside down. This offered a much faster rate of absorption by sending the drug directly where it performs it's task, the brain.

This would help to create a whole new breed of addict. However, not before Francis Burton Harrison, fed up with the addiction rates and the apparent inability to legally put a ban on the drug, found a loop hole for the time being.

It was through this loophole that they soon created what was called the Harrison Narcotic Tax Act. This new tax law had stated that only certain people would now be permitted to hold, carry, or dispense opiates of any sort. Were one to be caught in possession of *any*, it was now against the law, and so therefore they required a term that described just such a thing. For this, the term 'illegal possession' was coined. By 1923, half of all the inmates at Leavenworth Federal Penitentiary were there on some degree of federal drug possession charges.

By 1925, Heroin gets banned entirely, for medical *or* personal use. Morphine would now remain as the top choice for surgical pain relief, as well as for wounds (on and off the field of battle).

After banning it's use, the Chinese authorities, attempting to address a problem similar to the situation that they were facing here in the US, chose to deal with the issue somewhat differently. When handling similar illegal possession offenses, the authorities would publicly execute the narcotic offenders. Oddly, this was not the deterrent that one might expect.

Another issue that the US government soon found to be a problem, was that they were now noticing how many of the men returning home from war (the Korean war, Vietnam) were now *hooked* on opiates. This was largely attributed to the ease of access to the drug that the soldiers had had, either from medical kits or local abundance in whichever territory that they were fighting in. President Nixon decided to take action. He did away with the ancient tax laws regarding opiates, and appointed John R. Bartels as head of the newly formed FDA.

Nixon, determined to nip this thing in the bud, demanded that all US G.I.'s that were coming home from Nam, must now be evaluated and placed in rehab (if necessary) prior to returning stateside.

∞

Heroin was named after the German word *heroisch*, which means heroic or strong (from the Geek *heros*). It was chemically termed diamorphine, and after it's chemical analyzation in the 19th century it was found that most of it's uses were due to two alkaloids. The *euphoric* effects of the drug were the result of the diamorphine being converted into 6-monoacetylmorphine (a psycho-active metabolite) and morphine, which, then bind to the opioid receptors in the brain, effectively blocking the sensation of pain.

Contrary to popular belief, heroin *can* in fact harm the body after prolonged use. Recent studies express the various ailments acquired during and after prolonged use, such as; Hypnotremia, a condition that occurs when the sodium level in the blood is too low; Toxic Leukoencepholopathy, which causes damage to the white matter in the brain; decreased kidney function; fungal endocarditis; deep vein thrombosis; respiratory depression; abscesses; contraction of blood born pathogens (like Hepatitis B and C); HIV; anxiety; depression; and withdrawl, as well as a laundry list of other possible scenarios. It would seem as though a country that did *not* want it's youth to abuse opiates, would certainly want to educate them on these very things. Yet I had never heard about nearly *half* of these ailments when I was a teenager, let alone know that I could end up contracting one of them as a result of opiate *use*.

Research has shown that 80% of heroin users had begun abusing prescription painkillers before making the switch to heroin. As most will tell you, the pills can get extremely expensive, as where the heroin is always going to be far cheaper. Just to give you an idea of the vast market in this country concerning painkillers, it was reported that in 2015 pharmaceutical company revenues for opioid painkillers had reached fifteen billion dollars.

With legalization of marijuana in many states, the illegal drug production and smuggling operations, in an effort to replace lost profits, have now begun pushing cheap potent heroin into far reaching new markets. This has effectively created a rise in opiate related deaths nationwide, with rates in New England particularly high. This number quadrupling since 2001 at 1,256 deaths in Massachusetts alone (for 2014).

Each year 46,000 people die in the US from heroin overdoses. This equals to 126 people a day, 5.25 an hour, and 1.31 addicts dead every fifteen minutes (according to the FBI). It has also been found that 93% of those identified as needing treatment for dependence or misuse of an elicit drug believe that they do not need help. In my opinion this was the scariest data of all, because it brings to light the fact that just about every last person out there that is caught up in some kind of drug use is in absolute denial. The data is saying that out of one hundred users only seven are aware that something is not right. These are the type of mindsets that we as addicts must do away with. We must welcome all the help that we can get with open arms, as the day *will* come when there is no longer anyone around who cares enough to worry about you and your problems. This, in addition to the fact that you will eventually be just too run down to even help yourself. The result could be a lonely end to a rough existence. It is only once we learn to ask for help and accept it, that we begin to heal and change for the better.

Here in the US we have gotten accustomed to using one of two key medications (bupenorphine and methadone) for the treatment of addiction. However, there are some countries that have long been experimenting with these, as well as *other* methods *not* currently legal in the US, such as diamorphine (pharmaceutical heroin). This drug is administered to the patient twice daily at a medical facility, where the client is given a fresh syringe already prepped with a dose of pharmaceutical heroin in it. They then monitor the client as he injects himself, simply for the purpose of safety, and then that's about it. The patient returns two or three times daily, and avoids ever having to hustle drug money, commit crimes, share needles, worry about bad batches, or stress the situation at all, ever again. I have even read of one particular facility that has been administering pharmaceutical cocaine in *addition to* the diamorphine, allowing the patient to speed ball legally and safely. I'm not sure that this is rehabilitation, but interesting all the same.

Currently, these methods of treatment are used somewhat sparsely, in the UK, Germany, Switzerland, Austria, Canada, et al. In Portugal, recreational drugs such as heroin and cocaine are legal. This is a unique approach to the problem, and has caught the attention of politicians and researchers the world over. Analysts from countries all across the globe are watching the charts and figures in an effort to gain an understanding of the effectiveness with this method. As far as I've been able to gather, there has not been much of a noticeable difference as of yet, but the program is still in it's infancy.

There is another method that is also currently illegal in the US, which incorporates the use of a drug that is produced from the root of a plant found in one location only. Ibogaine, a naturally occurring psycho-active substance that is derived from the bark of a shrub belonging to the plant family known as the Apocynaceae, is found only in the villages of West Africa.

The ibogaine is extracted from the root bark of the Tabarnanthe Iboga plant, and prepared as a tincture that is said to have hallucinogenic effects. These effects cause the individual to adapt an introspective mindset, allowing the patient to make realizations regarding the true source of their inclinations to abuse elicit substances. Many individuals who have used the treatment have remained drug free ever since. However, there have also approximately seventeen deaths *allegedly* related to the treatment. The drug has been said to eliminate, or greatly reduce the withdrawal effects from opiates, thereby providing comfort and enabling the patient to focus on the roots of their substance abuse issues.

Over the years there have been conflicting reports regarding the Iboga. The African tribes that are indigenous to the area where it is found have been known to use the drug for ceremonial purposes for many years now. There are several Iboga 'clinics' around the world now that claim to be having some very real success with it, though seeing an Iboga clinic in the US anytime *soon* is probably not going to happen. This is to say, that, if you *are* interested in this type of approach, you will need to buy yourself a plane ticket and head to Africa (or one of the other countries where it is still legal to produce). One can find loads of information online regarding these clinics, as well as the info on how to access them, for those who are truly considering looking into it.

On to the Next Level

I sometimes wonder if I were given the opportunity to go back and re-live my youth, to do things different and that sort of thing, would I even want to? Each time I weigh the pros and cons surrounding the possibilities of it, I always arrive at the same conclusion, which is that *I* would prefer to just stay as I am. I appreciate who I've become, and although it *would* be nice to go back and avoid all of the strife that I have caused my friends and family, I feel that many of my trials and tribulations were necessary in my specific situation. As if this were all some twisted type of fate that was tailored specifically for the purpose of delivering *me* to adulthood. We all have different methods in which our life lessons are absorbed, and unfortunately 'living and learning' has been the theme throughout most of my own life. Besides, who would truly want to endure all of those trying times *again*, now that we've already made it through them?

I grew up a California dreamer as I listened to Jim Morrison beckoning me west with his enigmatic poetry, splashed over infectiously haunting melodies. The Grateful Dead had caught my ear as well, and had filled me with the desire to hit the open road. Just prior to my psychedelic era, I had taken part in the original suburban teenage Caucasian rap enthusiast movement. Which of course is not a real thing. It is simply the way I'm describing the occurrence experienced all those years ago, when many suburban white kids suddenly took to listening to rap music and dressing like gang members from Southern California. It was 1987 and I had purchased *The Beastie Boy's License to Ill,* and I can recall playing this cassette in my yellow Sony Sports Walkman as I would walk back and forth to the local retirement home where I had served meals as part of a community service obligation I was to fulfill, per our town's Juvenile Review Board.

NWA's Straight Outta' Compton had also come out just months after that in *1988,* and had completely knocked us all for a loop. My friends and I had become obsessed, for a time, with wearing all of the baggy clothes and different colored "Ewings" that were immensely popular at the time. These "Ewings," were rather expensive high-top basketball sneakers endorsed by

NBA All Star Patrick Ewing. They seemed to make them in an endless assortment of color patterns, and one who was comfortable going to the city (it was a big deal at that age) could certainly find some unique color styles. We were also constantly on the hunt for new rap to listen to. Back then it was not exactly easy to get your hands on fresh material, there just weren't that many rap artists out at the time, and the artists that *were* making music were (primarily) from the other side of the country. Hip hop was still in it's early stages, but it was certainly clear to everyone that this was something expressly unique.

Growing up as a kid in suburbia, we had lived in a somewhat large old house that was set way back from the road, nestled snugly in a quiet Connecticut neighborhood. Our big blue house was propped up on a hill, which one of the previous owners had actually done themselves while updating and adding a cellar to the home, sometime back in the 1800's. Using primitive tools, they would of first had to jack up the house, and, while leaving the house on stilts, build the basement underneath and fill in the remaining open area with loam or (fill). It made the home look unlike any other in the neighborhood, and I can see it now for the uniqueness that it had held. However, as a child I absolutely hated it. I can remember all of my friends having nice newly built homes, and this would leave me feeling as though we were in utter poverty compared to the other families. This was a distorted mindset that I had adapted as a result of a bit of bullying I had experienced, right up until about the age of sixteen.

I really didn't have much trouble finding friends as a child, but I *would* often try to mingle in social classes in which I did not fit the criteria. All of the neighborhood kids had dads who were fairly successful, and mine was the one riding past their homes barefoot on a motorcycle that otherwise sat buried in the back of our garage year round. He would dig it out once, most every summer, spend all day working on it in his bare feet whilst revving the engine, and wrap the day up with a ceremonial ride to the Mobile station for a pack of cigarettes and back again.

The bike was cool, but the bare feet drove me nuts. They inflicted the most pain when pulling up to the roller rink, 1987, in the '79 Ford LTD wagon. Dropping me off at functions such as this were always a family affair of course. Having three small siblings I was condemned to the "way-way" back, which was approximately forty or fifty feet from the front of the car. I would plead for my stepfather to bring the car towards the back of the building somewhere, and after sitting up from being slunk down, would find that he had pulled right up directly in front of the main entrance. Climbing out, I'd be forewarned by my stepfather as he jumped out in his bare feet and tattered jean cuffs, "Now that's my last ten dollars, don't go spending it on them God damned vid'ya games." And there it was. The way *my* mind worked, the entire 7th grade has now just made the one and only opinion they'll ever make about me, which is, we're poor, my father has no shoes, he's blasphemous, and he refuses to acknowledge the finer points of the English language. Oh, and my family treats me like spare cargo.

Truth be told, I happened to *like* the farthest region of our station wagon. I had the area all to myself back there, and I'd lean my head against the glass and watch as the scenery would continuously fall away from me. And my step dad *did* in fact own several pairs of shoes. He *was* somewhat of a hippie at the time however, with a pony tail and beard to go along with it. But that was not unusual for the era. Still in his late 20's to early 30's, he was relatively young, having just started a family with a new home that was quite large, in a very hushed neighborhood, as well as a brand new plow truck. The evidence would point to a situation that was far from the way *I* had felt back then, but that is how it goes for the socially awkward kid and there was just no getting around it. I did not come from money, I wasn't exceptional in any particular sport, and I didn't have the glamorous looks. Still, I wanted to be accepted by these preppy types so bad that I would repeatedly make attempts to fit in, only to have things blow up in my face time and time again.

Our home town was a suburb of both Springfield Massachusetts *and* Hartford Connecticut, and was essentially a sort of half-way point between these two cities. It was a great town to grow up in, with rivaling high schools as well as that one cop that all of the local teenagers would fear running into, Coop. Officer Cooper was this bad ass African American police officer who had wore an afro, and would always make it a point to put on a big show any time he was confronting a group of suspected 'ruffians.' He would then flex his muscle and let us know just 'who's town this really was' and that whole bit. Though he certainly did qualify as an asshole cop, you

35

could at least be sure of what to expect from him.

Our family consisted of myself, my mom and stepfather, and my three half-siblings (though we had never observed these technicalities). I was only two years old when my mother had divorced my father and remarried soon after, having two boys and a girl with my new stepfather. This hence left myself with the burden of being the oldest. My relationship with my family as I was growing up was great, and I was therefore left with many wonderful memories that I hold onto dearly.

Although my stepfather and I did tend to bump heads ever since I had been a toddler, we *had* learned as we had gotten older to put our differences aside. I did not dislike my stepfather, but I was an anxiety prone teenager who could not find comfort in my own skin. I was, of course, experiencing all of the angst and confusion that one encounters during the pubescent age. My stepfather had become an easy target for my blame, as well as vice versa. It is unfortunate that neither one of us possessed the skills necessary to communicate our thoughts and feelings back then, as addressing this problem certainly would have altered our situation for the better. I *am* thankful that we did have the chance to make peace, long before his passing in 2011. RIP DRB

I hadn't met my biological father until I had dropped high school at the age of fifteen, and my mother, who was looking for answers, called him and ask that he come over and speak with me. It's no secret that she was hoping he could help me to see the gravity of the decisions that I had been making at the time.

I remember I was told to go out to greet him in the yard, and when I had I had found this swollen up version of myself with a mustache. After having done five years fed time subsequent to his marriage to my mother, he had spent a lot of time focusing on bulking up, apparently. There *was* an issue however, he was in the grips of a terrible bout with alcoholism during this time (he has since been clean many years), and really was not in the best of shape to be setting an example. He also had his own business which had required his attention (and time) constantly. Although he *had* helped to steer me from trouble for a time, fate would surely step in soon enough.

36

This was sometime in the late eighties to early nineties, and kids at this time did not have the kind of access to information as they do now. I can't tell you how many times (nowadays) that I've identified with various symptoms of an ailment that I would learn of, and in turn concoct some unrealistic scenario in my head with terrors of terminal illnesses or psychological abnormalities. Then, after I'm sufficiently paranoid and racked with fear, I'll go online to learn that whatever it was that I had thought I was experiencing, was actually something far less dreadful. My point, is that you are now able to find out just what it is that you are going through, which more often than not is actually something that is quite common. Not that diagnosing one's self using internet searches is an altogether *safe* practice, but it can ease the mind of a hypochondriac with too much time on his hands. However, this can also create a hypochondriac. That being said, please do **not** rely entirely on information gathered from online queries. If you are unsure of anything, do the safe thing and consult a physician.

Anyhow, there would be no diagnosis for *me* at fifteen, yet instead an overwhelming feeling of guilt, loneliness, and low self-esteem. I subsequently began a process of beating myself up from the inside out, which was a routine that would continue over the course of the following two decades.

I did finally make it out west when I had turned sixteen. It was at this time that I had had a best friend from the neighborhood whom I had literally spent every waking day with. His name was Tom, and he and I had one of those friendships that transcended all others. Sometimes Tom and I could just take a ride to nowhere, not say a word to each other for hours, and have the absolute best of times. It was 1993 when Tom had gotten his license (before me) as well as his first car, a 1985 Buick Regal. To us, having a license and a car that would now take us away to anywhere but home, was an utterly glorious event. It was in those early days that we would often just suddenly up and take whatever we had for cash at the time and split town. We would hit the highway and just go with no destination in mind at all.

Tom and I did absolutely everything together. He too had an undying yearn to get to California and taste the road life just as I had, and so making the decision to dive *head* first into the whole "lot" scene had come almost instinctively for us. The "lot" is what the parking lot (pre, during, and post concert) tailgating was always referred to as, among those select deadheads who had come to live their lives on the road. There was a code among these "heads" that they shared among themselves, which of course created a family of sorts. It was a very tight knit culture with its own language, micro-economy, and hierarchy, and it was an interesting oddity for a couple teens such as ourselves.

So Tom and I saved up and bought ourselves a couple of round trip tickets riding on the Greyhound Bus Lines, all the way from Hartford Connecticut to Sacramento California, for $68 each way. You see, back then Greyhound had this promotional discount at the time that offered to take you anywhere in the lower forty-eight for '$68 or less.' There was even an accompanying little jingle that would tend to burrow into my brain like a parasite any time I would catch the commercial. We as teenagers didn't really have much money at all, and so if we were going to make it to California any time *soon*, this was going to have to be the way.

Well, I had never ridden a bus like this before and let me tell you it was sheer hell. Four days straight with *mostly* the same disheveled, unshowered and unshaven people the entire time. The bus began to take on a certain smell after the first day or so, and they had failed to trade it out for another one until we hit Des Moines Iowa. Still yet, in the end it was all an exciting experience that I had once crafted into a short story for an English assignment. This was back when I was attending a community college many years ago in Enfield Connecticut. My teacher and fellow students had just fallen in love with it immediately, and thought it was just such a 'great little story.' This brought on a situation where I was forced to present my story to a large audience of my peers. However, as nervous as I was about all of this, it was actually received quite well and I was glad I had gone through with it. If only I had seen things just a little bit differently back then, who knows where I would be right now.

By about the age of seventeen my friends and I had completely submersed ourselves into the psychedelic scene, which of course had me smoking pot and taking hallucinogens of various forms. This also led me to

38

go on the road, following bands around the country and making money by vending various items in the parking lots. Although it may not sound like much to the average Joe, to a teen who was discovering the world beyond his home town for the first time, it was everything.

I would go on to experiment with a vast assortment of drugs during this time, but it wasn't until I began to slow down that things would take a turn for the worse. My friends and I had all sworn that we would never touch the harder stuff (and most of us didn't, at least not to the extent that I would). But as we well know, for me things just did not work that way. I was on a different path, and I would soon show an unshakable determination to follow it.

This business of road trips, concerts, psychedelics, and all that comes with it was to be my lifestyle for quite some time, and it was having a less than positive effect on me physically. It was about 1993-94 when my health began to fail and I started to have episodes of bleeding ulcers. These ulcers had apparently been manifesting in me since the age of sixteen, though I had been misdiagnosed a few times before the doctors would finally get to the bottom of it. I even recall one doctor telling me that I might have Lyme disease. This of course caused a temporary scare before they were ultimately able to rule it out. Anyhow, after approximately two years of these episodes, attempting quick fixes and state of the art medications, and still nothing would plug the leak. It wasn't long after *this* that I would go on to lose approximately two thirds of my body's blood and had literally been brought to the brink of death. I was then hospitalized and operated on over the course of a couple of weeks. The surgeons were faced with having to remove all of the damaged portion of my stomach, which equaled to (roughly) half. This, in addition to removing the specific nerves that were *creating* harmful acids. I was told that it was these acids that were responsible for bringing about all of the ulcers that I was experiencing.

At the time it was unheard of for a young man of my age to have these kinds of issues. This, I'm certain, hadn't helped my feelings of being different. I was put on a strict diet and told that my days of eating just about all of my favorite foods were over. My life from that point on was to be that of an older persons, with an extra bland diet broken down into several meals a day, numerous visits to the bathroom, and the need to nap after eating (as digestion was not pleasant by any means). Well, OK then so we do what we gotta do, right? And that is how it went, for a while anyhow.

After a couple of years of carrying on like this, I began to experience this unknown pain in centralized areas of my body, and, try as the doctors did, no explanation could be given. I saw several specialists who each did multiple tests, and ultimately threw up their hands in confusion. It was at this same time that I was in the process of opening a small retail store in Connecticut with a partner.

Ours was a head shop that was done in a tasteful style, and was located right on our local state university's campus. Just in case your not sure, a head shop is a retail establishment where you can buy glass pipes and other smoking devices. So as you can see the location would *appear* ideal. Much to our surprise, however, it had turned out that we were also directly across the street from a high school. This of course became a problem in the eyes of the local community. It was merely a fact that we had just happened to overlook, and when all was said and done it would result in our downfall.

My partner, Damon, was twenty years my senior, and when he began to move large quantities of pot out of the shop I was under the impression that he knew what he was doing. Apparently I was wrong, because we did wind up getting raided by the state police. Although that would be a story for another time. Still a fine example of how drugs were shaping my life right from the very beginning.

Damon's side business would often afford us opportunities to indulge in certain activities that were still kind of new to me. What would happen is, people would bring Damon trades of *all* sorts. He was dealing in pounds and pounds of weed, so we're talking about some rather sizable street values. Most commonly the offers were pills. Large quantities of pills, namely Percocets (oxycodone) and Valiums (diazapam). Amazingly, even *with* my anxiety problems I still never did care much for the Valiums. The Percs however, well, they were another story altogether. It was a love affair from the word go.

Us, being the successful businessmen we were (ah-hem), we apparently felt as though we deserved to treat ourselves to a line of oxycodone up the snoot here and there. To *my* astonishment, Damon had the ability to do this while not getting caught up in any kind of a habit. But with me, again it was a different story.

I had reached this point in my life where I was experiencing a significant amount of discomfort, and had also begun to have these panic attacks that would isolate me from the world for, sometimes brief, sometimes not so brief stints of time. Although I *had* found that when I sniffed the oxy's, I began to come back out of my shell. Suddenly, like magic, I would feel as though everything was going to be OK.

I was now beginning to function again at levels beyond my normal abilities, or at least that is how it felt at the time. What I know for sure is that I was now able to get out of my own head and have actual quality interactions with literally anyone, girls included. This, being kind of a new thing for me, was obviously considered a big bonus as far as I was concerned.

∞

So it appeared to everyone that I had finally found the right medication (although none of my family knew what it was). Bearing this new found knowledge in mind, I set out to obtain my own prescription. This would prove to be far easier said than done. I was faced with timid doctors afraid to write scripts for pain meds without a terminal type of illness or an existing chronic pain issue. It was because of this that I had begun fabricating stories of injuries and lower back issues, tweaking them each time in an effort to yield the best possible results. I would go on to develop back issues one day, causing one to wonder of the irony.

The next phase would be doctor shopping, we've *all* done it. After I had learned the ways in which to manipulate the different physicians and health centers, I then proceeded to exhaust every possible resource that I could find: ER's, ambulatory care centers, PCP's, pain clinics, and street pills. No matter what I did there was never enough. One of the reasons for this being that I just couldn't help but hand them out at get togethers with friends. I was determined to have everyone experience what I was feeling, which is another tool this disease has mastered thoroughly.

Back then I did not have any health insurance, and so as a cash customer I chose to use a local *family* owned pharmacy. This particular pharmacy happened to be owned and run by a friend of *my* family, Garret.

Garret was just about the coolest little old guy ever. He would always fill all of my meds at cost, and whenever I had stopped in to fill a script, I would visit with him in back where the pills were and hang out while customers came and went. We would shoot the shit while he harped on about the "God damned politicians!" Though I knew very little about what he spoke of, I *could* relate to some of it. I liked hanging out with him. It made me feel important when customers would come and spot me back there. Things were a little different back then however, being that the pharmacies weren't as commercialized and polished as they are today, and so this kind of thing probably would never fly these days.

It was when I had a primary care doctor shut down my refills on the pain meds that I was taking at that time, that Garret had suggested I give this doctor friend of *his* a try. There was no way I could have been prepared for what would become of *this*. Garret made a call for me right there on the spot, made an appointment for me to be seen immediately, and then gave me directions to a medical office that he told me was right nearby. "How convenient" I can remember thinking to myself, and as it turned out it was actually only about a mile down the road from the pharmacy.

When I had pulled up to the address that I was given, all that *I* saw was a little white house. It looked to me as though it were a home that someone was currently living in. I was beginning to think that I was going to have to go find a phone (this was still the pay phone era) and get the correct directions, but just then a younger guy and girl exited the door of the little house and were heading to their car, so I made my way over to them and inquired. They struck me as somewhat more joyful than you might expect someone who was coming out of a doctors office to behave, but assured me that I did in fact have the right location, and then went hurriedly about their way.

I had never been to a doctors office in a house before, and the sight of the place was beginning to make me wonder. The building wasn't in too bad of shape, but it could certainly use a little attention cosmetically. I can remember it had that white aluminum siding from way back when, with random dents and rust creeping out from the joints.

Inside, the walls were done in a sort of 70's era wood paneling and everything was there for a purpose, nothing more. Thoughts of WWII German officer stations came to mind. The two girls working at the desk (who were also the nurses), didn't wear scrubs like I was used to seeing in most other medical offices. It seems that even the secretaries wear them *these* days. These ladies, instead dressed more casual in jeans and tees. They were very polite and professional however, and instructed me to fill out a couple of papers, the doctor would be 'right out.'

Soon enough, a gentleman hobbled out to the 'lobby' to greet me, and by the look of him I began to doubt whether he would even be able to hear me, let alone help me. This thought brought on by the fact that he had on these gigantic hearing aids with big tubes and knobs all over them. When he spoke, it was in a half mumbled sort of broken English, with strong (what I had guessed to be) German or Danish overtones. This proved to be accurate, as I had later found out that he was from Denmark, and just like many other immigrants his age, despite having been in the states for many years, never did manage to drop much of the accent.

He was clad in the classic white doctors coat that appeared a bit big on him, due to the fact that he wasn't very large in stature. This was so, to the point that the hem of the coat would sort of drag along the floor as he shuffled along. He wore thick dark glasses, had a balding white head, and liver spots all over. Were you to try and even his skin tone with an airbrush, you would have an easier time coloring in the areas without spots.

The lobby was not where the WWII theme ended either. The exam rooms were old and sterile looking. There were fixtures and instruments that were clearly from another time, and thankfully no longer got much use. The exam table was obviously designed to accommodate toddlers, having steps up the side of it, in addition to stirrups for delivering a baby (or a gynecology exam perhaps). The cabinets were done in that drab aqua-green that was commonplace long ago, with glass fronts where you could see all of the antique syringes, beakers, and hand crank centrifuges.

When the doctor came in the exam room, he took a seat on a stool directly in front of me (uncomfortably close) and explained that Garret had called him in regard to me. He now wanted me to give him *my* version of what was going on, and proceeded to stare down at the clipboard that he was holding as he sat, appearing somewhat attentive while I went on describing in detail the exact order of events and the extent of my discomfort. It's safe to say that he was asleep by the time I was (at least) half way through, and possibly from the minute I had opened my mouth. Anyhow, when I had finished my spiel, he sorta snapped to, shuffled some papers, and explained that I had only one option available to me if I were to stick with him, a new medication called Oxycontin.

I'll admit I did have a pill habit to some degree at that time, but this was what we would now call some 'next level type shit.' This was the late nineties by this time, and the brand name was still just about unheard of, which is a stark contrast to the household term it seems to have become today. Still, I had already known that the oxy*codone* worked for me, so it sounded hopeful. The doctor had forewarned me that the dose he would be prescribing today can never be increased, and if it wasn't sufficient, then there wasn't much else he could do for me. He wrote me a script for a weeks worth, gave me an appointment for one week away, and told me to come back for a whole months supply if I find that the medication helps me. Well as you might imagine the dose worked just fine as far as I was concerned, and so it began, a battle for my life and soul that would span the course of twenty years.

∞

At that time I was working for this little used car lot in Connecticut, as a driver slash mechanic slash gas attendant. This was the company where I was employed for a few years leading up to and after I had opened the head shop. It was a somewhat small used car lot, with a set of two antique looking gas pumps (with the digits that spun around like a slot machine), and a few garage bays for repair services. It was owned and ran as a family business, with the exception of myself and two others.

Their family name was the Panelli's. A very good natured (local) Italian family, whom, since that first day I had stopped in for gas and grabbed the help wanted sign from the window, treated me as one of their own and never questioned my actions. This was actually *too* convenient for me, as it had been before *their* eyes that I would eventually transform into a 'card carrying addict.' The thing is, we were all adults who respected each others privacy, and so they weren't about to put me out front like that and expose the elephant in the room, it just wasn't their place to do so.

The Panelli family was huge, eleven kids to be exact. Even with such a large family, they had all reached some level of success in their own way. This could be intimidating to someone like myself, being from a rather modest background. The gas portion of the business was run by one son, while the garage and used car sections were run by another. The patriarch of their family, Teddy, had owned a junk yard for the first twenty-five years of his marriage. This appeared to provide a fair living for he and the twelve others, as he had put every one of them through college. Try now, if you wish, and imagine a family of this size attempting to make it *today* depending on that same type of income. With things set up the way they are now, Teddy would of had to be a doctor slash attorney just to keep food on the table.

Teddy was a unique little character. He was maybe five feet tall, with a snow white head of hair and an angelic smile that'd pry any customer's wallet right open. He just had this way about him that you couldn't help but love. In his later years, he resorted to sitting in the service station all day, in the swivel chair, swinging this way then that, with the occasional (hourly I'm sure) snuff from the bottle in the back room. This, I'm assuming, was partly the reasoning behind the smile.

One night, he was heading home in one of the 'lot cars,' a '95 Dodge Neon to be exact, and, with a little shine on, had smacked a sharp curb head on and popped all of the airbags out of the dash, as well as left the front end with a dragging bumper cover. Amazingly, the car remained running and he apparently was unharmed because old Teddy just took to moving the deflated bags out of his way as best as he could and went on about his way home. The next morning the car was parked right back where we had had it, with the air bags bunched up and stuffed haphazardly back into the dash, and the 'for sale' sticker put back on the windshield. There would be no explanation given and nobody was asking either (though he *had* told *me* in confidence, everyone else knew anyhow).

Tone

Back when we *had* finally launched the head shop, I left my day job at the car lot to work full time in our store. Well, when the shop had gotten raided, I was hence left in a pinch regarding legal fees and whatnot, and so I had asked my former bosses sister, Maura, who was an attorney and court magistrate, if she could please help me out of the jam that I was in. She was an unbelievably nice woman, who had agreed to help based on a stipulation that I would go back and work for her brother (at least for a while). She had claimed it was because he really needed my help, as things weren't going too smoothly after I had left. However, I happen to know that while the Panelli's *were* supportive of my endeavor, they weren't too keen on the products that we carried or the partner that I had taken on, and she was more than likely just trying to look out for *my* best interest. The business was still a new venture for Damon and I and the attorney's fees would have wiped me out financially. So I had reluctantly agreed, though I was a little uneasy about how Damon was going to take it. As it turned out I was right to be concerned, as I would never again hold any real position at the headshop after that, and would ultimately split ways with Damon. It was clear things just weren't going to work out, and the loan that we had received to open the store was in *his* father's name anyhow.

While employed by the Panelli's, I had befriended the auto detailer who had been doing work for us for some time. He did *his* work in a bay that he had rented from my boss, located in the back of our garage. His name was Mike, and what was not revealed to me in the couple years that I had already known him, was the fact that he was a raging heroin addict who was now in recovery (or so he would say). The real truth was that he was actually quite active and was known to break into our garage at night and steal the cash for the next mornings drawer, as well as cigarettes and anything else that he could turn into a quick buck. The family would put up with his antics out of sympathy, which again kind of gives you an idea of the type of people the Panelli's actually were.

Mike had sold me Percocets on a couple of occasions before, but that was the extent of our drug interactions to this point. That is until one fateful day when I had come to work while in severe withdraw. The Oxycontin would prove to be far more in control than I had yet realized, and considerably more difficult to come off of compared to the standard Percs I had been used to. This made for some rough mornings, as I was trying to maintain a job while simultaneously maintaining this opiate habit. Anyway, I must have looked awful because Mike took one look at me and said "Your dope sick aren't you?" I conceded, and he explained that I didn't necessarily *have* to suffer like this, and so of course he now had *my* attention. Without much more talk on the subject he plainly said that he would take me to the 'city' after work, to which I promptly agreed knowing full well this wasn't for a ride to the detox.

I swear, I thought the day would never end. Many can relate I'm sure. Each minute that passed felt like an absolute eternity, but quitting time would finally come and as soon as it had, off to the city we went. As we barreled up the highway in Mike's '88 Lincoln Continental (his pride and joy), he gave me a quick (convoluted) tutorial on how dope is essentially the very same experience that I had been accustomed to, only, a little stronger and a lot cheaper. To be honest, I would have drank piss had I been assured it would help. By this time I didn't care how, I just wanted relief.

We took the Jennings Road exit, which is the North End of Hartford, and we met up with this Puerto Rican guy named Tone. He would go on to become my sole source of opiates for at least the next 6 months. Tone was a short Puerto Rican kid who drove a pimped out Taurus wagon, had a bunch of kids, and even more pit bull puppies. Well, maybe not more. I can't say for sure, but they were neck and neck. The puppies would tend to load his back porch with poop, and it was just so putrid. Especially in the summer time if I had to go inside and I was already kind of sick, ugh. I think he bred them for money, I don't know. I *do* know that he did it in a section 8 flat with no kennels. Tone was a humble dude though, and it was a little sad for me at the time when I had heard of how he had gotten robbed and then subsequently busted shortly after we stopped meeting up. Poor Tone right?

You see, Tone was selling $3 bags in a $5-$10 market. So it's safe to say that he had made some enemies by offering the same or a *better* product, at a drastically reduced rate. He was also well known to keep *all* of his cash *and* material with him at his home, and not in a 'trap house' like most other drug dealers do. Keeping all of this in mind, and factoring in the droves of white kids and shady looking urbanites that were rushing his door at all hours (in an area where white folks are spotted for *typically* one reason only), and you can conclude why the police soon took action. But this is how it goes and he will most undoubtedly sell heroin when he gets out of prison as well. Sad but true. (Don't shoot me Tone).

∞

Over the years, I have had one dealer who had gotten shot and killed just as I was showing up to meet him. Another one who had shot some random guy in the ass and caught a longer bid than many others have gotten for murder. Yet another one who had served these bags that were stamped with the name 'Take Over,' of which I had even purchased some myself. They were way too strong. Fortunately for me I was only a sniffer back then and only had about 30 bucks on me, because some ten plus people would end up dying from them. The bags were somehow traced back to Adrian (the dealer), with solid evidence linking him to the sales, and so *he* had gotten put away federally on several counts of involuntary manslaughter. The feds go day for day with their sentences, and so therefore what you get is what you've got. No good time of any sort, no parole or 85% type deals, and so, it is suffice to say that he will never see the light of day again. I have had hundreds of dealers over the years, and with the lifestyles that these guys (and sometimes girls) tend to lead, it's a safe bet that at least a handful have either met their makers ahead of schedule, or the inside of a prison cell.

∞

It wasn't long before I was cruising down the diamond lane to Hartford and meeting up with Tone at a minimum of once a day. I had been making good money for a while now and had a little nest egg saved up. However, it took no time for me to rip through that and then begin to spend other peoples money on *my* drug habit.

During this time I had met some friends of Mike's named Chris and Theresa. Chris and Theresa liked crack. I mean, they did dope, but *always* together with crack. Anyhow, we would sometimes get together and go to the city to cop heroin together. However, each time that they would begin to smoke their crack, they would try to get me involved. Like me, they just wanted to share the experience that *they* were having and were certain that if I gave it a shot that I would just love it. I politely declined time and time again and explained to them that I really only needed the opiates to dull the pain that I had lived with every day. While they did appear to understand, they still insisted on attempting to share with me *each* time. The funny thing about this is that when you *don't* want to try something, everyone wants to share with you, yet as soon as you decide that you *like* it the sharing is over and you are on your own.

I did finally cave in and opted to give cocaine and crack the old college try, and, while I wasn't crazy for it, I did appeal to the idea of being able to consume more dope without passing out. This would, henceforth, mark the next phase of my drug era: That being the span of time I had spent sniffing heroin and smoking crack cocaine. It was also about this same time that I had blown through all of my own resources entirely, and was now beginning to burn bridges on a daily basis. The crack brought utter chaos to an already volatile situation.

This is by far one of the lesser enjoyed side effects to crack, it's ability to suck up the cash at an alarming rate. You are stricken with a desperation that you must begin hustling for that next rock before you even *light* up the first one. It truly feels as though your life depends on it, and in some cases (as I will explain) it does.

The 'come down' from cocaine and especially crack can in certain instances be a catalyst for suicide in individuals who are already emotionally drained and susceptible to thoughts of this nature. This is why I chose to no longer get involved with it a long time ago. I had become a felon while in the process of trying to avoid that come down. In fact, my entire criminal record, which is lengthy to say the least, can be attributed to my fear of coming down from one thing or another.

My life until then had been one *almost* entirely free of all criminal activity, but for the act of buying and consuming drugs (marijuana), which of course still counted. As I turned twenty-three I was beginning a heinous wrath of petty theft and quick buck scams. Refund fraud to be exact. While I was attending my first detox, I had become friends with this guy named Jerrod who was from a neighboring town. His (drug money) hustle was a form of refund fraud involving a simple concept he had devised using sales slips. This method would yield cash right from the store, as opposed to what many others had been doing, which was to steal random items and then spend a bunch of time running around town trying to resell them. Jerrod had worked out *this* routine at one particular store, and then for some reason kept his focus solely on the one store.

During our stay Jerrod would walk me through his hustle, and had asked if I could give him a lift 'home' after we completed the program. I agreed, albeit somewhat reluctantly.

When the detox program finished, we had gotten picked up by my mother and my younger sister. This was, I believe, X-mas eve of 1999. We gave Jerrod a ride, and sure enough when we stopped at the grocery store for him, he went in, ripped them off and came out casually with cash that he had just received *from* the store (unknown by my family of course).

Next, we had my sister bring us to this random 'spot' in Holyoke that Jerrod was familiar with, and we went in and copped heroin with my family outside waiting in the car. I concocted some bullshit story about it being Jerrod's grandmothers house, and in retrospect I can see that nobody bought it. We left Holyoke and dropped Jerrod off at a park in Chicopee (which is another suburb of Springfield). He had said that his family was going to pick him up there, but I had my doubts about that story. Anyhow, we said goodbye, parted ways and I never saw him again.

I'll never forget the dope spot that we had gone to that day. The setup was one unique to that spot alone and it worked something like this: What you *first* saw was that they had a camera mounted on the outside of the front door. You were to ring the doorbell, at which time you would hear a bar slide across the door from the inside. You could then push open the door, and upon entering a voice would instruct you to close the door. When you did so, the bar came sliding out of a hole in the wall and blocked the door shut, obviously to keep you from leaving without paying. It kind of looked and felt like some type of trap that 007 would find himself in. There was a hole for the doorknob to the apartment, and all of the business transactions were carried out through that. After these faceless peddlers would receive their money, you would hear the bar then slide once again, and that was it. You were on your way.

Anyhow, little did I know just how much this one day would change my life. I was fascinated with this ability to get *cash* from a store, and then just walk out casually. No running, chasing, tackling, etc. Instead it was "Have a nice day!"

I studied Jerrod's method over and over again in my head before I finally gave it a shot myself. Gradually, I had found out that this trick worked almost everywhere. You would have to first find out what the store's return policy information was, then tweak your style to meet their rules, and bingo, free money any time you needed it. This was, again, a different time. These days the stores are plenty hip to this method of shoplifting and are prepared for anyone who dares try it. Back then, if they were to catch you they didn't even know *what* to charge you with, as they had not been subjected to these types of offenses before.

This hustle soon became my focus entirely. I made almost all of my drug money in this fashion, pretty much from that point onward. The up side to all of this was that I was really good at it. However, the down side was that I was *really* good at it. Until now there had always been a cap on my daily drug consumption due to lack of funds, only now there *was* no more cap as long as I was willing to put in the effort.

Looking Back

I have been figuratively dead three times that I know of for sure (there *were* some other really *close* calls). Each time that this had happened I was revived with the opiate antagonist drug naloxone, or "Narcan" as it is commercially known. I saw no white lights, no relatives from my past, and no eternal fires either. I was not able to look down and watch as the EMT's were working on me, or hear any divine spirits calling out to me.

As I looked back on this, it made me sad to think that maybe this time on earth truly is it. Perhaps this human existence *is* the end of the line. Yet, having wasted so much of it myself, I wanted more than anything to believe that this is not the case. While I was not raised with religion, I *have* always took comfort in the notion that someone or something *is* watching over us and hearing our prayers. I've just always figured that something as elegantly assembled as our universe could only be the work of one with divine abilities, the likes of which man could never comprehend.

I began to doubt many of the beliefs that I had once held. This, coupled with the fact that my soul had already sustained heavy damage due to my lifestyle being what it was at the time, meant that my faith in *anything* by this point was simply hanging by a thread.

Looking back, I can see that this was delusional thinking. As it turns out, I would now be considered by *some* as walking proof of a supreme being's existence, citing my recovery as a miraculous turn of affairs. The average Joe couldn't fathom the type of scenarios that we (as addicts) would subject ourselves to on a daily basis. There is no doubt in *my* mind that the series of events that had led me to this point have happened for reasons far beyond my comprehension. The places heroin has taken me, and the many people that I have encountered over the years of which I never would have experienced were it not for my addiction, these kinds of things can not always be simply written off as coincidence. I have managed to endure all of the obstacles thrown at me, amounting to something like climbing Everest. Just the fact that this book has made it into *your* hands or on your tablet, is a miracle in itself. I want to clarify that I am using words like 'miracle' and 'soul,' not in the Christian sense, but from a more *universal* standpoint.

However, this can only be miraculous if you use the information. If you are in dire straits right now, believe me I understand. I'm sure reading a book is not the most desirable of things to do, but please get *something* from it. Even if it's not for you there is certainly bound to be some portion of it that speaks to you.

The idea of spirituality in recovery seems to most to be a logical one. However, this is a big world full of people with their own individual ideals. What happens is there are some who do not feel comfortable mixing the two when first entering the world of sobriety. However, these people typically do not have the best track record when it comes to their *attempts* at sobriety. Is it *their* fault that they do not fit into one category of recovery? Definitely not. This is why I saw fit to try and present *another* angle. One that, if utilized properly, can and does work astonishingly well.

Over the years I have failed at countless attempts to clean up my act. I have been incarcerated for ten official sentences and approximately twenty in and outs, or 'pretrial' stays. I have been to numerous detoxes all over New England, as well as our local facility more than twenty times. I'm on a first name basis with each of their individual staff, in addition to the staff at the county jail.

I've made the tour around these parts when it comes to county correctional institutions, as I have been to three of the larger ones in this area. I had also had the pleasure of making a stop by Osborne Correctional in Somers Connecticut. Once called Somers Correctional, this facility is a level 4/5 maximum and sits firmly atop a hill that looks down upon six or seven other less secure facilities. It was less than two miles from the home I grew up in, and I can remember being a child and looking up the hill from the road at this massive old structure, and being told that that was where all the "murderers" were. This was actually the truth, as it *was* the prison that the state had at one time used to carry out (as far as I know) all of it's executions. Up until 1960, these executions were completed using the common method of that time, the electric chair. In fact, although it is a huge place, I just happened to be housed within feet of where that chair's impending victims once rested their heads (which was F block, I was in G).

The last man that they had executed in the facility was by lethal injection and his name was Michael Ross. Ross, was convicted and sentenced to death for the murders of five young girls and three young women, all of which were from Connecticut and New York. Nicknamed "The Roadside Strangler" by the media, Ross, when asked what he wanted for his 'last meal,' committed one last act of defiance and responded "Give me what everyone else is having," which was to say that he would not accept any special treatment. The menu that night called for chicken-a-la-king (which I can tell you from experience was certainly not special), and from that day on, any time chicken-a-la-king is on the menu and someone asks what is for dinner, the response will always be "Michael Ross."

Another interesting aspect to that particular prison, is that you can have a sentence of ninety days, while your cellmate could be doing 10 years. Imagine a guy who isn't going home for seven or eight years, listening to a guy who is going home *soon*, speaking of the 'things he's gonna do when he gets out,' or worse yet, complaining about the thirty days he's got left. Situations like this are dangerous in prison and someone who isn't hip to jail etiquette could really find himself in a bind.

Over the course of my life I have walked away and abandoned everything I had in the world at least ten times over. I've severed many family ties and burnt bridges at a fiery pace. I've had knives held to my neck on three occasions (that I can remember), and have been rolled for my money at least twice. I've been laid out and robbed right on the main street twice (both times in broad daylight, and once right in front of my little sister). There is no feeling more detestable than that of some street person's hands running through your pockets just as your regaining consciousness. Just thinking back on it now *still* creeps me out.

Throughout the entirety of my addiction I have probably injected tens of thousands of bags of "heroin," or, what was supposed to be heroin. Anything these guys (mid-level dealers) would put into those bags, I would inject without hardly *any* forethought or hesitation whatsoever. Often times these guys are very young, they want to be like the gangsters on the block and sell drugs, yet they have no clue *what* they're doing. I have found that they will put just about anything (from baby formula to crushed pills) in their heroin to serve as a filling agent (cut), as a way to fluff up their profit margin.

Another possible threat that I had also managed to somehow dodge was that of the contraction of Hepatitis C or HIV. There really isn't any explanation for why I had never contracted Hepatitis. I had 'ripped and ran' with hundreds of addicts who *had* been diagnosed with the disease, thereby putting myself at risk, and still I just never caught it. It is true that I never was one for 'sharing' needles, so I'm sure that had played a big role in defending myself from the disease. But there are always other potential ways of contaminating syringes and paraphernalia, and so one can never be sure. The only reasoning that I can deduce otherwise, is that it just wasn't the way in which *I* was meant to go. These days Hepatitis C is nearly curable and is no longer the death threat that it once had been back when I had first gotten into the game. Still, if one were to tally up the thousands of times I've shot up and never had an issue, the odds are simply unthinkable.

Why would I bring *any* of this up? It is just additional evidence to the fact that I have managed to continually defy the odds at every turn. It's not unlike the movie *Final Destination*, in which the main character happens to cheat death's design by a fluke, and then spends the remainder of the film dodging the (unseen) reaper's repeated efforts to right it's wrong.

Section One Wrap Up

An individual who is attempting to follow the suggestions throughout this book will want to check in here at the end of each section and make certain that the key points discussed are being addressed. Therefore, after completing the first stage the individual should be:

- Gaining an understanding of the history and science behind the substance
- Acquiring knowledge of potential side effects
- Realizing that there is no such thing as a hopeless case
- Learning of the various rehabilitation methods available
- Beginning to question what it is in this world that can inspire you to fall in love with life again

Section Two

Burt

It was early 2012 when I was called for a position through a local temp service that I had used a couple of times in the past. This particular service has a lot of one or two day gigs, you know, manual labor type stuff. Anyway, they had sent me to a location in downtown Springfield Massachusetts. This is my home city and so I know my way around it pretty well. It is where the rock band Staind began their massive career. You have most likely have heard of Killswitch Engage as well, who is from two towns over in Westfield, and the band Shadows Fall, who had some real commercial success some years back got *their* big start here too. Western Mass has actually been the scene for some of the heavier bands over the last *couple* of decades. However, not only has our humble city created a few noteworthy headbangers, but we have been the home base of many famous beginnings.

Springfield happens to be the city where Dr. Seuss first sparked the minds of young children with his awkward tales of misfit villains, and a shifty feline with a penchant for large head wear. I would sometimes wonder, those late nights when I would be hoofing it around the city, if ever the very panorama that I was seeing at the time was the inspiration for a tale from "Whoville." I grew up on Dr. Seuss books, entirely unaware of how close the author had lived to us. I can remember *The Pale Green Pants With Nobody Inside Them*, as being my absolute favorite book when I was small.

Springfield is the city that gave birth to the sport of basketball, and (oddly), we also have the city that delivered us the sport of volleyball, five minutes up the road in Holyoke.

A few facts about Holyoke, with one footnote in particular: it is *the* heroin 'mecca' around here. The city gets people traveling from all corners of the state, as well as Vermont, Maine, New Hampshire, et al. Our local newspapers and news channels are riddled with stories involving (generally) white suburbanites from all over New England and beyond. The stories have a common theme, and typically involve young adults who are getting busted as they try to sneak in and cop their drugs, and then make it back out of the city before being spotted.

South Holyoke is where I spent all of *my* money during the last few years of my drug activity, and I had never before seen a city like it. You can buy heroin no matter what time of day or night, without ever knowing someone specific or where to even go for that matter.

There was a long span of time that I was an active user and had no idea that the city was so inundated with opiates like that. I of course found my way there eventually, and had started going there throughout the last few years of my use. I can remember well the first time I had gone there to cop dope.

It happened to be one of those dry nights in Springfield and someone had mentioned Holyoke in passing. I was well aware that a lot of guys were getting their heroin there, and so I figured I would give it a shot. Holy shit, this was a level of street life that was unprecedented considering my own experience. There had to be twenty something different dealers hanging out in this little neighborhood park that I had been directed to, all of them pushing and shoving each other to compete for my business. Because of this, the prices were dirt cheap (compared to what I was used to) and the quality was much more potent (and dangerous) as well.

Even with all its bumps and bruises though, Holyoke *is* a beautiful city, rich in historical buildings with intricate, intelligent architecture. The more suburban sections have a fair share of scenic mountainous roads, a ton of million dollar plus homes, and a state of the art community college. There are also a couple of *prominent* schools nearby. In fact, Mount Holyoke School for Women is just around the corner in South Hadley, and, founded in 1837 by Mary Lyon, it is a member of the Pioneer Valley Five College Consortium which includes such schools as UMASS and Smith College.

Holyoke's 'riff-raff' is almost completely confined to the cities "South End" and "Flats," as they are referred to. When I was growing up, the town had the only mountain for skiing in the area (Mt. Tom), and is where I had spent most of my early years before all of the drugs. I was obsessed with skiing as a kid, and spent countless hours watching Warren Miller videos and daydreaming about someday skiing the places that they would be filming at. Mt. Tom would one day get shut down, for skiing anyway, and I had gone on to different pursuits myself. I did wind up visiting many of the areas that were in those films, though I was not there to go skiing. Instead I was there following rock bands around the country, and so I had mostly spent my time smoking pot, taking acid, selling 'Honey Browns' and bottled water in the parking lot, and seeing concerts.

Holyoke is appearing to go through a change for the better, and have begun to fight the drug activity with some new and innovative tactics, such as multi unit task forces for example. They had also been the first to elect such a young mayor, at twenty-two, who brought to the table a fresh new approach to issues such as rehabilitation, and combating the drug dealers.

So anyhow, that morning when I had arrived at the job site I had noticed that it was right next to the cities (Springfield) largest homeless shelter. I am no stranger to this building. Many years prior I was, what we'll refer to as, a part-time resident there. It wasn't that I didn't have a family and a home, I was just so ashamed in myself that I chose to live on the streets and avoid facing reality. What I would do is show up late night (off and on), when I couldn't find anywhere else to rest my head and it was far too cold out for a hallway or a parking garage. Other than that I had made it a point to try and avoid the place. The facility is nice and refinished *now*, but back then it was an absolute pit. Coincidentally, the director of the shelter's parent company, "The Friends of the Homeless," subsequently went to prison for practicing shady business tactics.

The job *that* particular day was interior painting and it looked like it was going to be relatively easy. The prep work had all been taken care of. The supervisor instructed us to take breaks often, with the reason being that there was very little ventilation in the area that we would be working in. That sounded like a good plan to me, the part about the breaks that is.

While I was on my second or third break, I had encountered a rather strange character who came over and sat under the shade tree where *I* would sit and take my breaks. This man just sat there for my entire break without saying a word, and I didn't really think too much of it at first. Yet the next day there he was again, under the same shade tree at the same time that I was on my break, and again saying the same thing, nothing. It went on like this for a few days and I had begun noticing that when I would go back to work, he would wait a few minutes and then just up and leave. By about the fifth or sixth day, I had to ask what it was exactly that had brought him there (if anything at all?).

He began by telling me that his name was Burt, or at least that's what he wanted to go by, and he then explained that he just happened to live there in the area and rather enjoyed this spot to sit and take a rest while out for routine walks. My thought at the time was that perhaps he was a little embarrassed by the fact that he stayed at the shelter and just preferred to not speak out loud about it, which of course I would of understood.

I'll admit he resembled Shemp from "The Three Stooges" quite a bit. Which, in case your not familiar, meant that he was a tall, husky man, with black and gray hair (that appeared slightly greasy). He was somewhere around the better side of 60, with a look of wisdom and a hint of kindness in his eyes. He was of the old school, and you could tell that he was the type that, with a quick shave and a little Vitalis he was ready for the day. After talking with him for a little while it had become clear that this random old guy here was actually very quick witted, refreshingly humorous, and overall cool shit. Where one might have perceived him to be a large bumbling old grump, I saw a bright, charismatic old soul (and somebody to talk to on my breaks). I enjoyed talking with him, and I found him to be a wealth of information on the wildest to the simplest of topics. We began routinely discussing a vast assortment of subjects for the time that I had remained employed there (which was about three months).

While on break *one* afternoon, I had stumbled upon a topic which I had found him to be suspiciously quiet about. It was while we were relaxing under that same big tree, by this point we were both having our lunches out there. It was as Burt was stretching his arm out to reach for a soda, when his sleeve had gotten tugged up just enough for me to make out a portion of what looked to be a tattoo on the inside of his right forearm. What struck me odd about this is that the part of the tattoo that I had been able to see, I knew it looked familiar and it was driving me crazy that I could not place why. So I innocently enough inquired as to the nature of it, and was promptly informed that, "Perhaps that is a topic for another time." I thought this seemed a little off, but I suppose I could understand. This guy really didn't know me very well at all, and so it *was* possible that he was just shy about such things. Still, I couldn't help but feel there was more to it.

Little did I know at the time, just *how* greatly I would be affected by our having met. Burt would lead me down a path of complete and total self-appreciation, and in doing so, many talents trapped deep within my soul would soon be awakened.

This was one of my earlier attempts at portrait art, and it depicts the memory I have of Burt when we first met. (Diluted somewhat by his uncanny likeness to Shemp)

Incarceration

I had recently watched an episode of Lockup Raw, the television show that takes you on tours through random correctional facilities across the country, and in this particular episode they were at the Essex County Jail in Boston Massachusetts. Boston is just an hour and a half away from where I live, and so if I'm going to watch one of these shows I prefer to watch these episodes best. So they happened to be interviewing a female heroin addict from Southie (South Boston), when they asked how she felt about her consistent recidivism. Her response caught my ear as she likened her situation to the Boston based television show "*Cheeah's*," as she put it, and explained how jail for her is like *Cheer's*: 'Where everybody knows your name.' This kind of hit home for me and reminded me of how jail, after a while, can get to this disgusting repetition that does at times feel comforting in some twisted sense.

I have, in an effort to help those who have just entered the prison system for the first time, included some information on what to expect as you embark on your journey *through* the system. But I do suggest that you also check out my follow up book, which should provide any further information you may seek.

I was just about twenty-three years old when *I* had first entered the system. As a pale white addict who was melted down to skin and bones and looking like a fish (with my cheeks sunken), I swam my way into general population for the first time without a clue what to expect.

When you first go to the county jail you are most likely going to be held on what's called 'pre-trial' status until you settle your case. You will then either go home or get sentenced. If you have no prior record they will usually let you out the first couple of times. However, if you've managed to pile up a rap sheet like I have, they no longer let you go home. Not on a *reasonable* bail anyway.

In *my* home county certain cell blocks are assigned for pre-trial inmates. These blocks house inmates who are facing charges of *all* sorts, and are unfortunately all grouped together while they await their court dates. These blocks house murderers, rapists, drug dealers, gang members, abusive wife beaters, pimps and addicts, like me. Only, I'm here on a shoplifting charge, and the guy in the cell next to me killed his wife and her lover with a hammer when he caught them in bed together. I believe they called him "Hammer Head Ted."

I myself have had murderers for cellmates more than once before, but I was well aware of it and OK with it. I had become friends with the individual, and had learned that these things are situational. Not everyone who goes to jail for murder is necessarily a bad person, but often can be, which personally, if I know they're a murderer and I get a bad vibe from them, then I just choose to steer clear.

I would like to be able to say that incarceration is effective, because if this *were* the case then I would have sobered up seventeen years ago. While I would agree that each case is different and not every person that has shot dope has lost complete control of their lives, to this I would remind you that these outcomes *are* inevitable, only, different people experience different paths. Many are on what we call 'the installment plan,' losing control bit by bit until they are on an all out drug run, sometimes lasting months or years.

The lifestyle does eventually catch up, and the addict is then forced to face the music, for, what typically becomes a grocery list of charges (often times with multiple cases). So the individual then begins serving sentences in accordance to the severity of their charges. The resulting imposed sobriety is crucial for the addict who is somewhat *fresh* and has never made it this far into the system. There will be many regrets and self promises late nights within the dark corners of that inmates cell as they break their habit cold turkey. It is right then and there, I feel, that the addict is once more at a crossroads of life. If he (or she) does not learn their lesson this first time, and the jail does not sufficiently instill any real fear, it could be, in some cases, years before they have another real chance to quit.

The individual would have to make the decision to never again even glance at another opiate or *any* other chemical mind altering substance for the rest of their life. Period. End of story. No exceptions! What can **not** happen, is, the inmate, not understanding the gravity of their situation, gets offered the chance to ingest some kind of substance while in jail. Then, not sure how to handle the situation, and vulnerable, the subject joins in the act thereby igniting a sort of 'pilot light' that will now stay lit from that point on until the day they get out.

Once this happens, the individual then becomes an inmate and no longer just a citizen visiting a horrible place. These guys (those who continue to get high while incarcerated) typically last only days (often hours) after incarceration before ingesting some sort of substance. What happens next is, of course, another drug run as well as a simultaneous crime spree, which for a time all seems to go well.

Nothing lasts forever though, and soon enough everything approaches a kind of 'bottle neck' situation where it is just no longer possible to continue on any further in this fashion. Something *must* let go. Then one completely random morning the individual wakes up sick, broke, and running out of hustles (with everyone around him fed up). This is almost always the set up, when, yet once again something occurs, be it the result of a desperate act or what have you, the individual finds themselves calling home from the police station.

They will more than likely be bellowing demands that someone must come *now* and bail them out. This is the result of the emotional attachment to the drug overwhelming the addict in lock-up and driving the individual to obsess over the separation. Typically, the addict early in addiction will have *someone* that will come down and bail them out if it isn't too much money. However, while this works for the first few times, there does come a point when there wont be anyone to get you out. Not, of course, when you are an absolute menace to society and it's just much safer for everyone, yourself included, to have you on the inside.

∞

While incarcerated, one meets a whole cast of characters and then some. If I only had known many years back that I would one day have the opportunity to retell just what I have seen and been through. Clearly I would have taken the time to write every detail down.

Back in 2010 I was nearing the end of serving time for a whole pile of cases that I had racked up while boosting analgesic pain relievers. I would take about 60-80 boxes at a shot, of which I would make three bucks a box. I would travel all over the tri state area, every day, cleaning various stores out of their pain/fever meds, and would then bring it all to this one fence (one who buys stolen goods) that I had had at the time, Raul.

Raul was a Dominican friend of mine who had owned and operated a bodega in the city, out of which he bought all sorts of items from me as well as many other hustlers. The story *I* had heard was that they would ship all of the merchandise back to the Dominican Republic where they sold the items in family owned stores at a reduced rate. He bought a vast assortment of different items, and always had the cash to pay no matter how many items I brought. This often amounted to several full garbage bags per visit, sometimes multiple visits in any given day. I even recall a xeroxed "shopping list" of sorts, that Raul had made for the regular guys like myself, as certain items would get *so* hot that you couldn't find them anywhere. Having a list of secondary items and their potential value had made this process much more convenient.

Raul would ultimately get pinched after I had been dealing with him on a daily basis for a couple of years. This was a pretty big deal at the time and I can remember him making the five o' clock news when it had happened. When the newspaper reported on the bust, the police department claimed seizing $50,000 worth of stolen merchandise that they had found stashed in the basement of the bodega.

Anyhow, during this particular sentence that I was serving, cases continued to roll in due to a database that cops and detectives use to share information on various busts and their perpetrators. Detectives from all over would soon recognize my photo as matching video footage from cases that they were investigating, and so they would then ask that a judge issue a warrant for my arrest. As these warrants popped up, the jail would bring me down, in to whichever court district the incident had occurred in, and I would then either plea it out, or sometimes, depending on what they had for evidence, they would throw it out.

So, one Monday morning I had gotten up and went to intake for a charge that had popped up out of Springfield District Court. This was a case that I had created by attempting to run a receipt at a local well known department store. When I had arrived at intake (where the jail preps you for court), they changed out my clothes and directed me to have a seat in the cell, per usual routine. While I sat in the cell waiting, I was talking to a couple of the other guys who had court that morning as well, when, all of a sudden an officer began locking all of the cell doors and went about bringing someone into the processing area who was from the P.C. block (protective custody).

As we all peered on, we could tell that this commotion going on was a little more involved than the usual pedophile or informant that mostly made up the roster *in* the PC block. This time was different, and as we watched, our instincts were proven right, because this was no snitch, it was clubhouse music's own "Stevie B" from such hits as "Spring Love," et al.

That previous Friday night, The Mass Mutual Center (our cities local civic center) held an event of various clubhouse acts, of which Stevie was one. Well, it turned out that Stevie had some skeletons in his closet regarding our little city here. Apparently he had once had a relationship with one of the local girls, and they had gone on to have two daughters together 18 years ago. The relationship unfortunately hadn't lasted too long, and he has since accrued a hefty amount of back child support. His ex must have seen that he was coming to town and decided that this was her chance to try and collect, what we later found out to be a massive sum. Springfield PD waited for the show to end and took him into custody.

With this occurring on a Friday, and the sizable amount of the back support at $420,000, this was enough to keep Stevie held for at least the weekend. When Monday came and it was time to go to court, Stevie and I were now going to be transported to the same courthouse. This meant that we would ride over in the same sheriff's van, along with maybe five other guys that were in the main compartment chained to me. While Stevie had to sit in the PC cubby that had kept him separated from us physically, we were still able to talk to him through the mesh caging. I should clarify for Stevie's benefit that he was housed in the P.C. area, not by his own choosing, but

75

rather the jail thought it best with him being a celebrity and all.

Anyhow, after he explained his current situation, he told of how he had recently teamed up with Johnny Gill out in Vegas and had been doing some regular shows out there. After some prodding from a couple of the other guys in the van, they finally coerced him into singing a few bars of "Spring Love" during the ride, which was both amusing and off-putting at the same time. Just picture the scene, if you will, six inmates of all sorts, chained together in a near pitch black cubby of the sheriff's van, on our way to court at 7 am on a Monday morning. While some guys are still fresh off the street and fighting off the dope-sickness, there were also one or two guys who didn't even speak English. As we rolled down the highway, the other cars around are entirely unaware that *Stevie B* is trapped in the back of this thing, serenading a bunch of inmates with "Spring Love," a song that at least I can say *I* was a fan of back in the day. I would venture to guess that most anyone who was around back then (and of age) would be lying if they said they weren't. It was just a massive hit.

It was cool to meet him and see him in the all leather pants and jacket that he had had on for the show, complete with the big white butterfly collared silk shirt underneath (remember, they had taken him right from the concert). I had never realized before how short Stevie really is, as he can't be much more than five feet three inches tall. He was really cool about his situation though, and was able to laugh it off for the most part. In fact, he seemed *more* interested in knowing what *our* days were like, being that I think this was a first for him. When we arrived at the court house he had this big city lawyer waiting on him. The attorney, who was this beautiful sophisticated looking Asian woman, had on one of those buttoned up power suits that conveyed an image of wealth. From what I understand she had Stevie out in no time.

∞

I was also at one time incarcerated in the Worcester County House of

76

Corrections in West Boyleston Massachusetts. Pronounced "Woostah house" by those from the area, this was an interesting place to do some time. Although some of their policies (at that time) could make for a rough road, in the end it had created a certain element of excitement

Take for instance one inmate that I had befriended, named Daniel. Daniel and I were housed together at the work release center, which was a section *of* the Worcester House. This work release was not unlike others I had been in. It was still a form of incarceration, but with some simple privileges that, when taken away can often feel like a much greater loss than they really are. However, this is the new prison system template for most of the country, which is the result of many years worth of research, countless studies, and ample subjects and institutions for the probing.

It was while Daniel and I were participating in the program that he had begun to make little comments to me eluding to the fact that he was "not supposed to be there," which, at the time I had no clue *what* he it was he could have been referring to.

Daniel would often go into great detail with me about the 'old days' of South Boston, or "Southie" as it is affectionately known to those who grew up there. He was about 55-60 when I had met him, and was one of the true old school *Irish* mobsters from Southie. When he was a young man coming up, he had hung around all of the heavy hitters of the time, such as James "Whitey" Bulger and Johnny Martorano (who has admittedly killed dozens of men and only served twelve years). When we would talk in confidence, there were times in which he would express to me the woes he had suffered from over some of the dirt he had taken part in throughout the years.

Though he was at one time attempting to go on the straight and narrow, Daniel found himself once again inside a Boston bank at the back end of a Smith and Wesson. This one particular incident had caught him a federal sentence of nine years. It was during the last stretch of *that* sentence that the warden had allowed Daniel to come down from the federal system and finish up his sentence at the work release, where I was. This was a sort of 'minimum move' for him, and I'm sure it was a nice break from the federal system.

While there, Daniel and I chose the same work crew, which is a five or six man team that goes out into the community and performs various manual labor tasks, such as painting the firehouse or raking the cemetery. It was at one of these work sites one *random* morning that the drama had quickly unfolded.

The days leading up to this had been a little awkward between Daniel and I, as he was dropping (what I later had realized were) hints to the fact that he was planning something. Each morning when we would go out to work, he would bring this huge wad of postage stamps that he had acquired during his stretch in the feds. Postage stamps, if you didn't know, are the main currency among *all* inmates in federal lock-up institutions, as well as many state run facilities. The inmates use these to gamble, buy drugs, and barter, and the *idea*, is that they are the only item that stay one value, on the streets as well as in the joint. That, and the fact that an individual can turn them into cash whenever they *do* get out of prison. He had shown me these on this one particular morning, sort of letting me know bit by bit that he was on the verge of doing *something*, but I couldn't make any sense of what and I wasn't sure I even wanted to know.

So we headed out that morning, off to work as usual. It was Daniel, myself, two other inmates, and the deputy that drives the van and keeps an eye on us. The job that day was located at an outdoor recreation area in a nearby Massachusetts town, installing an entire jungle gym type set for children. It was a $64,000 set up, so this was no small job.

We were working with the town's Department of Public Works, and so we were all using their equipment, such as the backhoe, auger, bobcat, and some assorted hand tools. All of the guys were grabbing tools off the truck as they needed them, and with all of that movement going on, Daniel was given the window he had apparently been waiting for.

As I was running the auger with one of the other inmates, drilling holes into the ground for support beams, I hear, "Whoa, hey, WHOA! LOOK OUT!," and then turned to see Daniel peeling out in the town DPW truck, almost hitting a woman who was power walking a stroller as well as some guy who was attempting to jog by. Daniel had laid a strip from where the truck was parked, straight out the gate and down the street.

Despite the Sheriff's Department having a "spy" placed just across the way (to keep tabs on us and the officer who watches us), Daniel managed to flee with the vehicle and drive it all the way to Roxbury Mass, which is a suburb of Boston.

He had ditched the truck by the time they had found it, and was obviously long gone. After this had happened, I kept thinking back on the things he had said to me, like the fact that they had never retrieved the money in one of his bank cases (of which there were many). This meant that it was still an open case, hence the reason he was not supposed to have been allowed at a minimum security facility, I'm assuming anyway.

They did catch up with Daniel fairly quick. It was only four days later in a motel somewhere up in New Hampshire, and the rumor at the time was that he was found to be (allegedly) with a prostitute, some crack, and a fair amount of cash. Now, one can only speculate, but it would appear as though he still had some of that loot lying around and was determined to get out and get at it.

Daniel was just one of thousands that you cross paths with while serving your time and getting shuffled around the system. Many of these people are smart, talented, and full of potential. Often the kind of potential I wish I had myself. However, prison is not a nice place, and so what happens is, in order to survive, the inmate adapts to his surroundings and lets the negative aspect begin to take control of his thought process. From there, it's a tough road to get rid of it.

The county jails hold all kinds. The strong, the weak, the smart *and* the stupid. But therein exists a collection of alpha males amongst them. The court system attempts to weed out the lesser offenders with short time and time served, while the more *imposing* offenders, the one's who are seen as an actual *physical* threat to their community, tend to receive harsher penalties and longer sentences.

The more timid guys that do receive long bids, will typically catch on quick. Which, in other words means, the minute you know or even think that you know that you are going to go upstate: right then begin doing whatever you can to get your weight up, engage in an effective workout routine, and do not get involved in *anything* you can not handle. This is necessary. There are no two ways about it. If you want to survive in prison, this is where you start. Oh, and do *not* gamble or allow anyone to spot you anything.

I say all of this, because the state prison is where all of those alpha males from each and every county wind up, crammed together, all competing for top dog. While it is unfortunate, very ugly things happen to good people all the time in these prisons.

Every now and then an individual falls by the wayside, and *is* able to exist in prison and go virtually unnoticed. I have known a rare few to pull off this kind of status, and am reminded of one in particular who had decided he that had had enough of this [prison] bullshit and he was gonna do something about it.

His name was Jeff and we had played a lot of cards together. Other than that I knew very little about him. In fact, all that I truly knew about him aside from things learned through idle chit chat, was that he had a home, a wife and a couple of kids. He was my opponent (in card games) usually, but we seemed to get along just fine. He was a quiet younger guy who just wanted this time to go by and get it over with. Especially *one* night, after making a phone call home to his family and expecting his wife to answer, had another man pick up *his* phone at *his* house. I guess he felt that certain suspiscions that he had apparently already had were confirmed, and so in *his* mind he simply had nothing left.

After playing cards that night, Jeff cashed out of the poker game, went up to his cell, and with only days left to his sentence, hung himself from the top bunk with a rope made of bed sheets.

If it were not for drugs, that man and thousands of others would still be here today. These situations are such a waste of life and are an absolute travesty. We are getting played like fools as we are picked off one by one (either by death or incarceration).

∞

One can learn a lot by observing a jail or prison from the inside. There are many aspects that either just don't get addressed, or simply don't translate well to television. Many believe that since they've watched these lockup type shows, they feel comfortable in committing crimes of various magnitudes, assuming that they know what to expect (should *they* get sent to prison). I am here to tell them that they have not gotten the full story, of this I promise. I have been witness to countless acts of severe violence while incarcerated. I have seen random guys get jumped or just plain beat down, bad, just based on one inmates word that the person was a snitch or a pedophile, or in certain instances, an ex-gang member that is 'green lit' (which means that all other members of that gang have a green light to inflict violence and are mandated to do so).

At least 6 out of 10 times the information is inaccurate, and an innocent man (of the inmates claims) gets, often times severely hurt. It's for reasons like this that many guys *join* gangs. It is typically the younger ones, who are effectively scared, and so it looks to be the best option for them. It's about power in numbers. They see a group of gang members all hanging out together, appearing well respected, and decide that they want that life. The problem, is that these oaths that they take are for *life*. Blood in, blood out as they say.

I have rarely (if ever) seen a forty or fifty year old gang member who does not regret his decision. Typically, by about age 30-35 they begin to understand that this is no kind of life for an adult and start to look for a way out. One option many seem to take nowadays is to turn states evidence, which is a legal term for informant or snitch (as they say). This is kind of a tricky topic to cover. As one who had lived this prison life for so long, I now have personal reservations which are distorted due to institutionalism. These mindsets acquired in prison have been the hardest of all to shed. The issue with being a snitch, is that it is a stigma that an individual will carry with them for the rest of their life. If they were to ever find themselves in prison again, in order to remain safe they would have to spend the entire sentence in solitary confinement. Be it known that these prison gang members have ways of finding out *everything*.

Another common trait that I have observed, is that almost ten out of ten times the biggest baddest guys in the joint who throw their weight around (trying to inflict fear before ever having to prove themselves) will almost always be the ones with the sketchiest charges, the shadiest backgrounds, or simply can't fight worth a lick. This is often all part of a premeditated act meant to divert focus and avoid having dangerous secrets found out and the like.

There is also one other scenario that this type of individual can be sure to engage in. If he happens to be indigent (no money for commissary), he will work out constantly, and attempt to use his size for purposes of obtaining food and other commodities by way of bullying the more quiet (timid) guys. Any of you that have done time know exactly what I'm talking about, and any of you who haven't but *might* do time, watch out for these effin' weirdos. Some of you may have even been that guy, which is fine too.

Thankfully I personally had never run into these types of problems, but I *did* have to fight a time or two. In fact I'm forever scarred as a result, having received several stitches in my face after my first scuffle. I had learned quick the ways of this little world, and found that it isn't altogether difficult to get along in prison, but it *can* get complicated. It's just too many personalities (guards and staff included) packed into such a small area for such great lengths of time.

I had always made it a point to have my *own* hustle going on, and it was because of this that I had had a mutual respect with most of the guys that I had to live with in there. I had taught myself how to cut hair, which is a big money maker in institutions such as these as well as an important service for the inmates. This was actually one of the many skills I was forced to develop throughout my incarceration history. I had stumbled upon this hidden talent purely out of necessity, however, I soon found that I didn't mind cutting and it made the days fly by. I would cut my own hair (using two mirrors), and then little by little I had picked up tips along the way. Here it is twenty years later and I now can produce a quality comparable to that of the guys that work in the shops.

When a man has had an issue with recidivism and cannot seem to last out on the streets, we typically call this being 'institutionalized.' What these terms mean, recidivism, institutionalized, is that the individual has been locked up or in treatment for so much of his life, that it has become his lifestyle and he has all but forgotten how to exist out in society.

One would assume that once the need and the desire for drugs disappears, then so does the instinct to hustle. However, as the ex-con attempts to rebuild his life, it takes a great deal of effort to exchange this negative thinking for positive. It sounds simple enough, but has proven to be anything but.

If you are coming out of prison and are trying to get clean, it's not unlike being up against the proverbial 'two-headed beast,' as you must first put yourself through a *rigorous de-briefing* of sorts following your prison term. Then, and only then, will you be able to adequately *combat your addiction* and begin your new life.

The Pike

So it was another frigid night in Western Massachusetts. My girlfriend at the time, Jess, and I have run out of drugs and are soon going to want to brave the elements. Though I know for certain that there is very little gas in our car, I'm not quite sure *how* little. The gas gauge does not work so we really haven't any idea *whats* in it. I had been using the odometer to track the mileage, as we knew the distance the car could make once the gas light had popped on, only this particular night I had lost track somehow and so it was a crap shoot whether or not we could make it to the 'block' and back. Bear in mind it's also midnight in the peak of New England winter. So we took these things into consideration and off we went, naturally.

Back during that time in which my life had consisted of one ridiculous scenario after another, there were literally countless incidents that could stand as perfect examples of the ferocity with which I had been destroying myself. However, there were certain incidents that had left a bit more of a lasting impression. This was one of those times.

It was approximately a fifteen mile trek to the dope spot from where we were staying at the time, but mostly a straight shot down the (Mass) pike. I believe it was 2009 and I hadn't had a license since the nineties. Yet I'm behind the wheel, of course. Jess *did* in fact have a license, but the problem was that this car (Chrysler Concord for those who care to know) had absolutely no brakes whatsoever. I mean nothing. I had even wore out the emergency brake down to straight metal, by keeping the handle pulled out while using the pedal as if it were a regular brake pedal.

The method I would use to stop at *this* point was utterly ridiculous and highly dangerous, for us as well as the rest of society. It went something like this: First off, I would drive *really* slow everywhere we went, of course, and would then immediately let off the gas the very second that any hint of a stop sign or red light could be seen ahead in the distance. I would then glide until we were slow enough that I could begin throwing the gear shift (automatic) into Park repeatedly, causing us to slow down in very small increments.

Dink! Dink! Dink! Is the sound that we would make as we slowly inched our way toward the red light. Approaching the light, I would continue to do this until we were just about slow enough that I could then *slam!* the shift all the way into Park, stopping the car abruptly and rocking us violently too and fro.

It was all quite a spectacle and often times it wouldn't work. It would then turn into a situation where I was forced to cut the wheel, jump the curb, and attempt to steer my way out of it safely and without damaging anything. Although I did manage to keep everything safe, I would try and play it off like everything was cool, when the real truth of the matter was that nothing was cool, especially me.

Sure enough about half way down the turnpike we found out *exactly* how much gas we had left, none. So there we were on the side of the road (who knows where), at one in the morning, with no gas and no filling station anywhere in sight. The pike has strict rules regarding unattended vehicles, they tow them, immediately! I had left a car once before parked in the breakdown lane while I went walking with my gas can, and twenty minutes later came back to find the tow truck passing me by with my car on the back. The tow driver tooted the horn and waved to me as he passed by, so I *know* that he saw me with the gas can. However, if he were to pull over for me he might have felt morally obligated to give me my car and let me put the gas in thereby missing out on the tow/impound fee.

Understand that this is how the local tow companies make their money. They patrol the highway like vultures, in hopes of spotting a vehicle left for dead. That is when they move in for the kill. Acting swiftly, the car is yanked onto a flatbed and hastily carried away to jail (impound lot). Bailing it out typically requires a small fortune. So with that being said, it's always best to stay with your car and wait for assistance.

Now, I can't just leave Jess alone out here while I attempt to seek out some fuel. It being late and dark, I just wasn't comfortable with it. She was a very cute kind of girl, perfect prey for some creep I'm sure. So we made the decision to sit and wait for one of the emergency/rescue vehicles to come along, hoping they might have a gallon of gas with them.

So we sat, and we sat, and it wasn't looking good. All the while running our hazard lights to draw attention, in turn killing the battery, and it was then that things really seemed doomed. That is, right up until a pair of headlights pulled up behind us. Excited and anxious, I went to open my door when a stern voice suddenly barked, "STAY IN THE CAR!!" Now if I was to try and describe my expression at *this* moment, you might think of a blow up doll with that sort of wide eyed "Oh shit!" face.

Regretting my situation more by the second as we nervously waited, when, up to the window walked this big, Smokey the Bear hat wearin' behemoth of muscle, bullets, and tasers.

He said "Whats goin' on tonight?," while bending down to look in and see Jess' face as well.

I shakily proceeded to explain the situation regarding my gas gauge, the hazard lights, etc. While I'm stumbling my way through this explanation, the thought enters my mind, shit, I've got no license, an active warrant (maybe), paraphernalia in the car, and I'm in the driver's seat with the keys in the ignition. What the hell was I thinking leaving myself posted here like a sitting duck?

However, to our amazement the officer was surprisingly good natured and *very* understanding. There would be none of the usual routine, we've all heard it, "Where were you going?," or, "Anything in the car I should know about?" To the contrary, he informed me that it could be another hour or two before an emergency van made it's way down there, but that he himself was willing to try and help. He explained that his car had a push-bar on the front, and he offered to give us a shove two miles up to the rest area. We knew that they had gas there, we just hadn't realized how close we were in proximity to it. So I promptly agreed, and off he went to his car.

He was soon lining up our bumpers and the next thing I knew we were moving at a speed of (roughly) 60-65 mph. Each time we reached 65'ish, he would give a good shove and then back off until the momentum would begin to wane. As we approached the rest area we could see the beautiful glow of the fluorescents that we'd normally associate with food and fuel, and then it was one big push and we were on our own, rolling up the entrance ramp at 65 miles per hour, no brakes, remember, and no lights whatsoever (dead battery). So up the ramp we went, a dark, silent, blue mass of steel speeding in one side of the pumps...and...out the other side. Unable to stop, we glided all the way out to the highway and down the road a little way. It seemed to take an agonizingly long time for the car to slow to a stop.

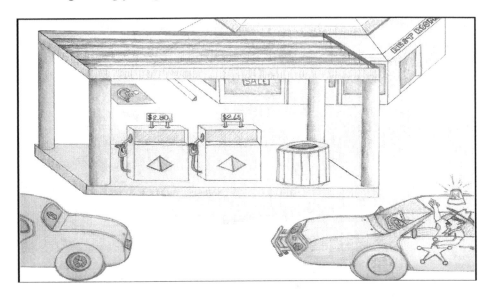

The trooper freaked out, sped up behind me and jumped out of the cruiser screaming, "What the fuck happened?!" I felt like a deer caught in the headlights. I steadied myself and said that I wasn't sure, but I think that maybe because the battery was dead this caused the brakes to fail. Of course this was complete bullshit, but if he thought that the car was unsafe (which it clearly was), he would of *had* to tow it, and we would of been stuck right there where we were. He bought it, I guess, and told me that I was on my own now and to just walk back to the station with my gas can. When I turned around to thank him he had frustratedly sped off without saying another word.

As I made my way toward the station I immediately spotted the emergency guy sitting in his van at the rest area and eating some McDonald's on his break (I assumed). After some pleading I managed to convince him to (reluctantly) give us a jump. This particular gentleman had given us a jump once before and it was an absolute mess. I believe I had to swap out batteries with an old one that I had kept in the trunk, or something like that. Anyhow, when I saw that it was him I kind of thought we might be screwed, but he finished his food and pulled his van around to our car. I poured the gas in, we jump started it, and that was that. We were now on our way to the block once more. Not back home where it was safe, but to a city that was miles in the opposite direction at two in the morning with a broken car.

It's baffling for others to try and comprehend just what it is that would compel a person to endure such a consistent series of calamities? The average Joe would have repaired the gas gauge when it had first broken, and the brakes at the initial sign of excessive wear. The addict, however, becomes oblivious to the world falling down around him. It is *the* truest form of tunnel vision one can experience. Whether it's the mission to make the money for the drugs, or it's the mission to get the drugs, either way it's a mission. It's *always* a mission. Oh, and God help those who stand in the way.

Beware

If you are *not* an addict and never have been, then I am going to advise that you beware. There are thousands of addicts out there right this very minute, careening through the streets with broken vehicles, no licenses, and open warrants. Often times they've just stolen something or pulled *some* kind of scam, and are therefore in a hurry. They could give a shit about seat belts or traffic laws, as they steer with their knees down the fast lane while simultaneously injecting speed balls. Now, I would like to clarify that I mean no harm by making these statements, I am simply reporting the extreme nature of what I have experienced.

Some heroin addicts have a penchant for ingesting large amounts of benzos (benzodiazapines), taking them *while* shooting heroin and causing the individual to fall asleep just about anywhere. Please note that this type of addiction model is *the* utmost dangerous of them all (among the opiate world), and should be avoided at **all** costs. Please, if you do not have a solid understanding of drugs or prescription pills, let me tell you, mixing benzodiazapines and heroin is by far the deadliest combination that you can find. Heroin overdoses occur when the brain fails to get oxygen due to the lung's inability (respiratory depression) to pump the air in and out. This respiratory depression is a side effect of the extreme sedation, and it kills addicts all across the country on a daily basis. This is able to occur as the individual becomes too sedated to realize what is happening, and hence, literally forgets to breath. So with sedation being a key factor here, and knowing that a strong benzo such as Xanax is intensely sedative on it's own, then you can deduce that when the two become mixed, what you then have, *essentially*, is the stuff that kills rock stars.

There are *other* heroin addicts of yet a different breed. I am referring to that of those who are on 150 plus milligrams of methadone, enabling the active addict to shoot coke or smoke crack throughout the day, while still being able to pass out at night ('night' being a relative term). However, there are heroin addicts that don't get involved with cocaine, and instead inject large amounts of *strictly* heroin. These individuals make it a point to

91

broadcast this ideology, as if to be implying that the cocaine or crack is beneath them. The idea here is actually a common one, "Well, I might be a heroin addict, but at least I'm no crackhead!" This ridiculous notion has been known to exist the other way around as well, where the crack addict looks down upon the heroin user.

Still yet, there are those addicts, who, by luck or sheer will power manage to maintain some level of habit and not fall into this kind of mentality. This book speaks to those of the highest use caliber and all levels thereafter. If drugs control some aspect of your life, there *are* words just for you mixed within these pages. Find the words, find yourself, find success.

Supplies

When you decide that you are ready to give this recovery bit an actual solid effort, understand that there are some items that one can obtain fairly easily with which you can benefit from throughout the recovery process. These supplies will ultimately become essential in order for this transition to go as smoothly as possible, and this is why Burt was so adamant from the start about this important action.

First of all, pick up a cell phone if you don't already have one. Then commence to loading every name and number of every positive person you meet from this point onward. The concept here is quite simple, to build a network of contacts to reach out to when various situations arise. Rides, information, a helping hand, we all need help at one time or another and therefore learning how to ask for it and accept it will be cardinal in your success. As life starts to take shape, it is important that the individual in recovery makes a respectable effort to establish new friendships and acquaintances with those of a more positive nature. You should also do some light house keeping when it comes to *old* friends and others that are perhaps *actively* 'using,' whose numbers may still be lurking in your contacts. Delete them and wash your phone clean of these evil elements.

Make certain the phone that you choose has internet access as well as an mp3 player. Which (nowadays) simply means that any smart phone will do. Music is going to become a big part of this process. As you push onward and are up against various tasks of difficulty, using music as a mood stabilizer of sorts will help to make any taxing situation go far more smoothly (especially in the early stages). However, if you are not a fan of music, which I suppose *is* possible, then download some audio books instead. Personally I prefer to be learning something if I'm listening to an audio book, but you will soon figure out for yourself just what it is that suits *you* best.

The plan, initially, was to suggest that you also have a television (most everyone does anyhow) to use as a learning medium. Our public libraries are packed with thousands of DVD's that are often informative and educational, and making use of all that is available to us will help to increase our chances of success. As far as television is concerned, however, I would recommend watching all of your entertainment selections online. Television can be an addictive and counter productive use of your time, believe me I know this to be true all too well. TV network executives have gotten extremely good at keeping you drawn in so that you may view more precious advertisement. George Orwell once wrote that "advertising is the rattling of a stick inside a swill bucket," which *does* just about sum it up. If you were to ask me, I would say that TV's are dead. When we watch online, we select what we want to see when we want to see it. While there are definitely still efforts to keep you watching, at least with the internet you've got to make a selection, which, by itself can be the difference between sitting through another program or getting up and doing something else, *anything* else.

Next, be sure to have a comfortable pair of sneakers. I myself prefer hikers, but whatever your preferred style is should be fine, as long as they're comfortable and have at least *some* tread. You should be planning on putting in some time out walking, taking in the fresh air and scenery and allowing yourself to expel any negative energy, while at the same time letting the positive in. This is a peaceful, oddly productive act that can change the course of our lives.

Let me explain. Let's say your in a troubled situation, on the brink of acting on an impulse and possibly doing something that will surely make things worse. Were you to pause things right there, stopped what you were doing and taken a short walk, this would *typically* be just enough time to calm down and see the situation from a rational point of view. By taking that short walk, you've in turn avoided acting out your negative impulses, and thereby saved yourself from potentially catastrophic consequences. I know it sounds simple, and that's because it is just that simple.

The next item you will need to obtain is a library card, that is to say if you don't already have one. The library is an immense wealth of information, education, entertainment, and tools for aiding in your success. While you should begin right away borrowing books to read, this tool will also become absolutely necessary when you begin the sixth and seventh sections. I will show (*in* sections six and seven) how an individual can find inspiration for an idea, create a solid plan, and launch and run a small business using only tools found in any public library.

The fact that your reading this book is a good indication that your comfortable taking time to read each day, and possibly a regular patron already. However, rather than doing what some other programs might have you do, and read the same repetitive thing religiously over and over, Burt instructed *me* to get myself a wide variety of topics that interested *me*. You should start with fiction if you have a hard time getting into books at first. Then, once you've established a routine, begin to pick up some nonfiction topics so that you may educate yourself and find which topics inspire you deep down. Perhaps you might find something that could offer up explanations for any personal situations that you may want to address. Also, I would just like to clarify that this was not meant to say that one can not learn while reading fiction. To the contrary, in fact, most fiction novels are bound together by factual information, thereby adding substance and a sense of possibility to the plot.

Fiction *does* have an important role in your reading, as it helps to spark the imagination. The very act of imagination is like a lost art to an addict, especially one who has been fully ensconced in the street life for some time. At this level there often isn't much hope left within the individual, who is effectively left in a dangerous state of mind. To imagine something better, they must believe in the potentiality of a straight life. There has got to be some shred of possibility and wonder that remains deep within the addict, and it is through this whole process that we locate it, dust it off, and put it to good use.

Hood Life

The "hood" is a crazy place to say the least. Daytime, nighttime, no matter *what* time it is, one is sure to find any number of misfit characters lurking about. Still yet, it is the families and children who live in these relentlessly tense, dilapidated areas, who are forced to carry on their daily lives beneath this dark cloud of negativity that seems to permanently enshroud the neighborhoods. This negative aspect appears now to have been woven straight into the fabric of the hood's very existence.

When an individual such as myself gets involved in the process of copping drugs on a daily basis, they find that unless there was an existing heroin connection among their own circle, they are soon wandering the 'ghettos' of their local city's neighborhoods in search of one. I happened to embrace the scene in the hood for a time, and before I had come to live in several of them, I could be found popping in and out throughout any given day. During this time spent crossing the line of battle (with drugs) back and forth, one can bear witness to a smattering of dangerous, bizarre, and sad situations.

It is at night that the fake smiles of the sunlit hustling and bustling daytime commuters and commerce patrons all but disappear entirely. This is when all of the local businesses, those who must treat their customers and clientele with some degree of respect, commence to closing down for the evening and conclude another day's transactions. As the sun dips lower, the slime of the hood's "third shift" comes seeping slowly out of the cracks of darkness to punch in and begin the night's activities. Liquor stores, bars, pimps, drug dealers, and convenience stores suddenly appear to spark with life (if you would refer to it as such).

For the most part, people encountered out here during this time are usually just making an effort to get through whatever it is they are looking to achieve, while doing it quickly and being left alone in the process. When observed from an outsiders perspective, one could liken it to the way in which spiders and mice inhabit our homes and apartments. These creatures live side by side with us while attempting to remain unseen. Similarly, they just want to meet a goal and keep as many others as possible completely unaware of their presence.

When thinking back on the extreme nature of my surroundings during this time spent abusing drugs, I am often reminded of an incident I was witness to one October afternoon as I was attempting to cop heroin on a small side street in the North End of Hartford Connecticut (sometime back in the early 2000's).

As I had turned off of Albany Avenue and onto Center Street, I was on foot and looking for a particular Spanish gentleman whom I was familiar with. Per standard routine, I was making an effort to move swiftly and keep to myself. The sun had just set and it was getting cold rather quickly as I was continuing to make my way up the street. It was pretty quiet, but for the low rumble of an import car's performance exhaust that I could hear coming up from behind. I looked back to see a Honda Civic with blacked out windows come slowly creeping up the way, and I can remember glancing back but had thought very little of it. At this same time, a teenager riding a bicycle was coming toward me from the opposite direction, and then passed me by riding a 'wheelie.' Now, when the Honda had gotten maybe sixty feet behind *me*, the kid on the bicycle was just about passing them, when just then, POP... POP, POP!!. A sharp sound of gunfire suddenly cracked through the autumn sky. I heard the exhaust now turn from a low rumble to a sudden whine as the driver (clearly) had dumped the clutch. The shots had sent people in every direction, screaming and ducking as they ran, and it was then that the Honda came speeding past me. I turned to look back, and saw that the kid that was on the bicycle was now laying on the pavement with the back half of his skull missing. There was a mass of blood all over, and no movement or signs of life at all. That child, I found out afterward, was only fifteen years old. He was also the wrong *child*. I had learned that the gang members that had shot (and killed) him were actually looking for someone else and unfortunately mistook him to be that individual.

Just for the record, yes, I did still go two streets over and purchase heroin immediately after witnessing this awful event. This is the ugliness that you *will* encounter, should you remain to be involved in this type of lifestyle. Were it not for drugs, I, more than likely, would never have laid eyes on so much, if *any* of this type of activity, and here I have now seen several dead bodies among countless other tragic events as a result.

∞

Life in the hood is a vastly unusual concept. It's cheap. Everything holds a substantially lower value here, and the human soul is of no exception. An individual can obtain most anything they would need or want, if they know where to look for it. Stolen cars, weapons, computers, electronics of all sort, clothing, food, cosmetics, medications, drugs, and various discount services are all available at a moments notice for those in the know. These "services" can range from cheap backyard mechanics, electronic repair, and manual labor, all the way to insurance scam artistry, muscle for hire, and murder.

These neighborhoods are predominantly occupied, ran, and patrolled by the local gangs. However, they must also be patrolled by the local police. It is no secret that most of these cops often have but little *true* power out here. The majority of them will pass through and make their presence known, while no doubt hoping there is no actual tragedy that would require them to have to get out of their cruisers and do some work. Although, every now and again a rookie *will* come along who is of a more aggressive mindset. These are the younger officers who tend to have a bit of spunk within them, and are the ones that I myself would always do my best to steer clear of. These guys (and gals) are of course trying to build up their reputations as well as their stats, and so *they* are going to be the ones who would be more apt to make the 'petty' arrests. In other words, these are the arrests for charges that many other officers would more than likely turn a blind eye to.

It was only recently that I had been passing through one of the local hoods here, when a pedestrian had drawn quite a bit of attention as he was

99

crossing the street in front of a city patrol car. This happened to be right there on the block in a heavily traffic'd drug area and known gang territory. Anyhow, the gentleman stopped and proceeded to flip off the cop while blocking the officers path to get through. He then began to taunt him by screaming "What, motherfucker," in a way that was clearly meant to intimidate. While he did this, he was flailing his arms and hands about and making a scene so that everyone around could see just what was going on. This had obviously been an attempt to demean the cop even further, and I was beginning to wonder how much longer the officer was going to let himself get punked down before he actually did something. This particular jaywalker had then even went as far as to make a "shooting" gesture at the cop with his hand, which *I* had thought for sure was going to be the last straw. And yet still nothing. The officer just sat there smiling demurely and waited for this guy to go on about his way.

While this could be written off as the result of an officer who is simply picking and choosing his battles wisely, it still represented an interesting contrast to the way in which life exists in suburbia.

The System

Have your ever heard the phrase "You can't beat the system?" Well I have learned from experience that this is all too true. I had found this out in the same fashion that I had come to find most things out, the hard way. However, I had also learned that in this life there are a number of different *types* of systems. Each of these systems have, to some extent, their own 'agendas.' And one in particular has an agenda which is all too sinister. This system starts the very first time you encounter a mind altering substance. Sometimes it's a life long process, and other times it's a rapid succession of events. Each one playing a vital role in the destruction of the subjects mind, body, and spiritual self. This system acts with stunning precision and without any prejudicial dispositions whatsoever. You might say it is an equal opportunity evil.

This system has quite a track record too. It has been relentless in its pursuit to destroy as many lives as possible. To stand up against it is a feat of will not meant for the amature. If you are new to recovery, then you *are* the amature. Hypothetically speaking, it's got you in it's sights. Assuming you truly have a problem, then I assure you you are in the most dangerous of situations. Something similar to pushing a large boulder up a steep hill. There is a good chance that you wont make it and will undoubtedly suffer more damages in the process. This system does have flaws though, and there are a number of loop holes and secret passageways out of this, if you know how to find them.

Fortunately for you I *have* found them, or they have found me? Either way, I would like for everyone to be able to benefit in the same way that I have been allowed to. So what I had decided to do was put everything I had learned over the years regarding addiction, down on paper. I then poured over numerous notes and journals that I had kept, and did my best to record the bulk of my sessions with Burt down on paper as well. Next, what I did was I researched all of it, as well as anything else I could find, which, once I had gotten going with it, it had turned out that there is a mountain of information regarding this affliction. But of course there is, there is also an endless list of it's victims.

After carefully examining all of the information that I had gathered, I then compiled it all together and subsequently separated it accordingly into seven sections. This being pursuant to those of which Burt had written and taught me about. Each section as vitally important as the next. What your reading here is the culmination of this project, and as I will show you, right away this proved to be something very unique and effective.

I have come a long way to get this information to you, please use it and use it wisely. Let's all together become as one, to move ahead and begin a new chapter to this story of pain, isolation, destitution, guilt, poverty, need I go on?

I have cheated death, misery, failure, depression, and a host of other attempts aimed at destroying me. My experiences have shown me that nothing is impossible as long as you possess the will to make it happen. I had once read about this old German doctor who was also an expert hypnotist, who had said, "You cannot leave your thoughts and wishes at the abstract level. You cannot vaguely want something and get it."

My success alone is proof of the possibilities that exist for even the most hopeless of cases. I have spent a good part of *my* life in the city, sleeping in hallways, abandoned buildings, and parking garages. I have eaten from dumpsters, pulled cigarette butts from ashtrays (or the ground), panhandled, and committed crimes on the daily. It's been a long arduous haul, but I've managed to scratch and claw my way up out of that hole, even as the dirt was piling on top of me.

These days I live in a much more *peaceful* setting, right next to a prominent New England prep school. Our town has an average annual household income of just over 100k, and the average home here comes in at just under 400k. While I *myself* am not a rich man, I've got plenty of big ideas and the drive to see them through. You see, writing this book is my way of helping the next man. Which is to say that I am still on the path just as well, and so my efforts here have become paramount in securing my *own* sobriety. What I *do* have, is friends, family, and peace of mind. I was *the* absolute, hands down, least likely person to get it right and straighten out. What I have accomplished can only be taken to mean that, with hard work and careful planning, any addict of any caliber can be successfully transformed into a new person, nearly unrecognizable to even the closest of family members.

Role Models

This is going to be one of the most important tasks when beginning your own journey to freedom. Freedom from having to fear waking up knowing that you are going to have to hustle yet once *again* just to get off 'E.' The premise of this chapter is for the individual who is seeking to make use of these concepts to understand that they *must* choose a role model. As mundane as this may seem, to properly utilize the suggestions in this text an individual is going to have to look for inspiration from others. Let me clarify that you do not have to necessarily settle on just *one* role model. One approach to this concept is to take *certain* attributes from several potential subjects. While these actions are necessary, they mustn't be discomforting. Seek out what inspires you to reach new heights and be everything it is you want to be. We all have moments of envy. It's human nature. No matter *who* you are, there has certainly been someone at some point that you'd wished you could be more like.

Which is precisely what this principle is all about. It's about showing you that you *can* be more like this person or that one. We're just borrowing attributes from those who have come before us and succeeded in life. We as addicts in recovery would be foolish *not* to do so. When picking up the pieces of a broken life, the addict finds that the rest of the world has quite a leg up on them, as not *everyone* has been preoccupied with the rat race of substance abuse as we have. Therefore, why not make the most use of any and all opportunities to up your chances of success. Success in recovery as well as in life. Perhaps utilize the time you spend reading as an opportunity to learn about some of the various great men throughout history, and what *they* did to attain such levels of success.

If you truly want to give your family the world as I do, then this is an important component regarding this particular way in which to do it. If it's what you want deep down and it will make your life more enjoyable, then you *must* do whatever is in your power to emulate the traits that you wish were your own.

One road block often encountered when attempting to practice this principle is your own ego. Our egos are powerful. They can often times keep us from living the lives that we want to live. One example of this would be a situation that had occurred while attending mandatory church services at a residential program I had once been in. As I would attend the services, I would be making efforts to try and fit in by imitating what was I observing others around me doing. However, I would get this feeling that everyone around me knew damn well that I had no clue *what* I was doing, and a rush of anxiety would then wash over me as physical discomfort set in. It was just this notion that I would get, that all eyes were on me, watching my every move. This would, henceforth, spark the idea to leave the program and I did just that.

Although all of these feelings that I was having were obviously imagined and completely fictional, when I put it in retrospect I can see that it was my ego that had been holding me back. It was that over exaggerated sense of self-importance that the ego *has* been known to conjure, that appeared to be the culprit in this particular scenario. It seemed such a shame too, I honestly wanted to embrace the church at the time, yet I let myself get in the way. These are the types of things that Burt had opened my eyes to, and, while it could seem so irrelevant at the time, when looking back I can see just how important it truly was. Had I been able to overcome these feelings from the beginning, things very well may have played out differently.

Who's the Boss?

It was springtime 2013 when I had taken a job with a local manufacturing/distribution company as a temp worker in their facilities maintenance department. I had worked for this particular company on a part-time basis a couple times in the past, but this was the first full-time slot I had been given here. This particular job happened to be a huge opportunity for me, when one takes into consideration that of my criminal record, spotty resume, and minimal *official* experience (some of the jobs I had had in this field were under the table). It had also come at a time when my family was in serious poverty and a chance to get a job that could turn into a career was inspiring to say the least.

I was truly excited to think that I would now be able to provide for my family, with a job that I love and that is right around the corner from my home. When I met my new boss Kip for the first time, he had explained to myself and two other gentlemen who were just starting out as well, that, although this was (officially) a temporary assignment, there were definite opportunities for those who made the effort and showed that they really wanted it. I took this idea to heart and made it my entire focus to impress them with quality, efficient work. I wanted this job. I needed this job, and I was determined to go to great lengths to get it.

So for several months my work days had begun something like this: I would come in, punch in and greet my foreman Steve, and he would grunt something mumbled back to me. Steve was a heavier set gentleman with a gruff persona that he conveyed to everyone (excluding his boss only). He specialized in the handling of dangerous gases and chemicals and had quite a few guys working underneath him.

He appeared to be a good enough guy from the start, yet as the days wore on he began to show signs of discontent towards me more so than others. It was after a one on one meeting that he and I had had, where I explained to him the fact that I was an addict in recovery and that I was determined to make the most of this opportunity. I don't know why I ever even said it, but once I had there was no turning back from it.

No matter how hard I would work for Steve, making *him* look good in the process, he just would not warm up to me at all. In fact, he then began to be downright rude, snubbing me in front of anyone he could, I guessed, in an effort to show others just how much he did not like me. This was going to be a problem, because there were positions opening up soon and it was nearing time to assign one of the eligible candidates, i.e. myself or the one of the other guys I had started with. I should clarify that throughout this time I had not missed one day, where the other two guys had missed several (with one even taking a week off with no call!). Now for *me*, this permanent position meant that I would soon be receiving a benefits package, more pay, IRA's, 401k, etc. While Steve had told me in confidence that if I put in the work he would stand behind me when the time came to select someone for the job, it was obvious he was scrambling for reasons to exclude me from being chosen. Still, he would give me special assignments which *he* had claimed were my opportunities to prove my worth, like cleaning the roof of the whole facility by myself (in the peak of summer time), or tending to the entire properties landscaping. *My* thought was, if I kick ass at this how could they deny me when the time came?

Just as I had been doing, I broke my back trying to impress and earn the respect of my superiors. Which I had. Even Steve admitted to me (again, in confidence) that he respected my work ethic. However, it was clear that he still did not like me and was not interested in my attempts to smooth things out.

After a while with things carrying on like this, Steve was laying out the instructions for us each day and getting overwhelmed with it all. This, in conjunction with the multiple million dollar projects that he also had going on at that time (at least that's what he told us). What he decided to do was have a third shift facilities maintenance worker, Rob, start coming in the daytime to work *with* us and possibly help to take some of the load off.

Steve's thought, from what I understand, was that since the two of them knew each other so well, he would give Rob the daily instructions, Rob would relay them to us, and we would *all* execute the specified tasks throughout the day. This was an easy enough concept to grasp, and it made perfect sense. However, there would soon prove to be a flaw in the setup of it.

Steve had never really specified any ranking between us and why would he of? He was the boss and we were the workers. Though I had soon learned that not everyone saw the situation in this same light. Apparently, Rob had decided on his own that we needed a sub-foreman, and then decided to assign that title to himself, again on his own. Considering the fact that he clearly had the seniority, there *was* some logic to the idea of it, and would have worked out just fine had he any common sense at all, though I assure you he did not.

Things only got worse from there. It took no time for me to realize that both Steve *and* Rob were going to do whatever they could to keep me from getting a permanent position. I was devastated by the thought of this. I had truly done everything I could to assure that my work exceeded their expectations, and what I was getting back was not the desired result at all. I had never had a boss tell me that I was working *too* hard. Who has? But that is what I was told time and again by these two, and it didn't make sense.

Scientific Spirituality

It was after I had met Burt that I had made the decision to seek out a more *scientific* outlook with my recovery, in the sense that there was some technical reason that was responsible for my lapse in judgment. I would like to clarify for the 'twelve steppers' out there that I *do* in fact subscribe to the tradition of establishing a higher power. However, as Burt has taught me, this does not need to be so close to the top of the 'to do' list.

Instead, take it rather slow. Let your higher power find *you* as you navigate your path to success. When your actions begin to start producing actual results and your lifestyle has been drastically rearranged, only then will you have the capacity to truly communicate with your God. In the early stages there is just *so* much to do, and your head is still 'in the clouds' (due to the drug's half-life), that it just makes much more sense not to worry the mind with such matters yet.

Don't get me wrong, as your body works to cleanse itself of the toxins, emotions will be sporadic and at times can spark moments of enhanced spirituality. This is of course a good thing. It is the connection to the spiritual world within you that is beginning to break through these barriers and defense mechanisms that have been put in place by the addictive behavior. "Don't take these moments for granted," Burt cautioned me, "it is a good indication of the fact that this world has a design just for you. You are still here with us for some reason, and it is your job to create a positive environment that will hopefully solicit further positivity in return, and in effect, enabling you to find your way."

If you are anything like me, then you are going to prefer as well to understand the nuts and bolts of addiction and how it pertains to you. I proceeded to educate myself in the more scientific treatments, while keeping a firm grasp on what works for other people also. I myself was not raised in a particularly religious home, and really wasn't shown to seek God until I had landed myself in treatment for the first time. This was one of those situations where I was desperate for a treatment bed, as is usually the case, and was presented with an opportunity to stay at a local residential treatment center. I knew nothing about the place, aside from things you hear in passing, as it *was* a large, well known facility.

Even during the intake process they made certain to let me know just how committed they were to preaching the word of God, which was fine by me. I had never experienced this kind of setting and wanted to give it a fair shot. Well it didn't take long for me to realize that if I was going to make it *here*, I would need to completely alter everything I thought I knew about myself. I was always a quiet, reserved person, and these new experiences were now causing me to feel really awkward.

∞

Burt put it to me like this, in order to take a scientific approach to recovery, one must learn the science of the substance and then the science of the abuse. What *I* had found, was that I was also going to need to learn the science of my own anatomy. This is where I had truly benefited the most. By understanding my body and how it works, as well as the causes and effects to all of these discomforting symptoms that I had been experiencing. Some of these symptoms which I had been suffering from since my teenage years.

When I think back to the beginning, back when this snowball first started to roll, I find that I began my drug seeking behavior in a search to feel better. Something was wrong, and instead of finding the cause I found a way to block the *effects* of the cause. What this meant was that I literally had to start all over again. It was as if I had been mentally on pause for the last twenty years.

This was OK by me. I had been miserable for such a long time by this point that going back to the beginning was an all too welcomed process. Essentially this would mean that I could, and would need to, start *everything* over. It's like when we were younger and were asked "What do you want to be when *you* grow up?" Well, the idea here is that it's time now to grow up yet once again. Only, this time it's going to prove to be quite a different process. This is where the information I am providing here is going to become the most useful, as I have personally been through all of this to the extreme.

When one spends two decades, as I have, in and out of jail, treatment centers, detoxes, and on drug runs, there just isn't much time left for education. Although I *had* attended three separate colleges over the years, I had never obtained a degree. I was, hence, left with the mindset of a twenty year old and the education of that of a well informed high school freshman. In my own defense I had spent a lot of time grabbing at any chances I could to learn and reading a lot of fiction and nonfiction while in jail and prison. Also, back when I would be on drug runs, running around hustling (drug) money, I would (unfortunately) shoplift books any time there just happened to be a nearby bookstore. Sometimes if I was in a pinch I'd hustle the money *from* the bookstore, sadly.

The point I'm trying to get across *here,* is that I was severely limited on knowledge about my own body and what it was that could have been causing so much discomfort all of these years. This is when I had really put into action my plan to start fresh and gain knowledge of everything I could along the way.

∞

The more thought I had put into everything, the better the outcome. I mean *everything.* For instance, I had never really had a good grasp on what foods made me feel what way. Life had been so chaotic there just wasn't ever any time to notice such things. The closest I had *ever* come to a balanced diet was whenever I had been incarcerated and the calories were counted for me. And even then I would wind up eating a lot of Ramen noodles and other junk food from the commissary. Still, I have found that when one does focus on a healthy and nutritious diet the resulting health benefits can help with numerous ailments. You've got to learn how to read labels as well as gain an understanding and get up to date about general nutrition.

Another good example regarding ailments that can alter your quality of life, would be posture and the resulting effects that an individual can be faced with after years of *having* poor posture. I had learned that the list of symptoms pertaining to problems with the spine can go on and on and on. Pinched nerves can create a host of symptoms, many of which are things I never would have considered the issues that I had had with my *spine* to be the culprit. A pinched nerve can literally affect every region of your body, and they are very common. So keeping that in mind, it would be a good idea to get *yourself* thoroughly checked out just in case.

One more example, and this was one of Burt's pet peeves, is water. Hydration is an all too important and often overlooked component to a healthy body. Especially a body that is bouncing back from a less than ideal lifestyle. I recently made the realization that I had not been taking notice of the types of beverages I was drinking throughout all of these years, and the contents therein. It soon became clear that I had been *de*hydrating myself even further with the beverage selections that I had been making. As a result of this, I have now learned that it is extremely important that I take notice of exactly what it is that I am putting into my body. And so basically the idea here is that you are going to want to drink a fair amount of water. You can research what is available for fruit beverages, as far as which ones are not going to have a negative effect, but water is always going to be the safest bet. Most nutritional guides will tell you to drink 6-8 8oz. glasses a day which can seem like a lot, though I assure you the benefits are going to outweigh the small struggles you may have to endure.

You very well may find that you have begun *your* addiction as a means of quelling some painful ailment (physical or mental) as well, and perhaps could benefit by searching within *yourself*, shedding light on, and attending to any areas in need of attention.

∞

If *I* hadn't gone with a more technical approach in seeking my own sobriety I never would have made it. Perhaps if I was a church going citizen prior to my issues with drugs, I would have found the same results down a different path. But I wasn't, and I didn't, and not everyone feels at ease with religious activities, not at first anyway. The name of this game is change. Even modern science established *it's* first shaky beginnings as a means of seeking a closer connection to God. Although the two have since become to *some*, complete political opposites.

Section Two Wrap Up

The individual should at this point:

- Have a better understanding of what incarceration is truly like, as well as its inevitability for the active addict
- Be able to recognize the lunacy of these turbulent behaviors from an outside perspective
- Be aware of what supplies are going to be essential in assisting you through these transitional times
- Begin routinely walking as a form of mood management, meditation, exercise, and a chance to get fresh air
- Starting to read as much as possible from a vast variety of topics
- Start thinking about potential role models and what attributes you would like to attain
- Realize that spirituality is important, but not urgent
- Begin to look within your physical and mental self for any possible ailments that may have attributed to your addiction

Section Three

Burt's Bamboo

Burt was a cryptic soul. He was one who could never remember dates and times regarding things like doctors appointments, yet he never arrived late for a meeting with me. In fact he was always there *before* I was, which could make me feel like a slacker sometimes. As if I were lacking commitment through my tendency for tardiness. As time went on though, I had learned that it was this kind of thinking that had kept me in the state I was in for so long.

He claimed to have little use for money and blatantly refused to *ever* accept any gratuity or charity. He would put on this little show anytime someone did try to give him money, as if to be setting straight any uncertain notions those around him might of had regarding his ideals. To me it seemed as though Burt was perhaps locked in some lost time, back when he maybe did have to do such things, and I would then feel a little sad for him (of which he would not approve I'm sure).

Burt was not one for the home life. He did have a family at one time, though any efforts of getting any information about them would be quickly shot down. He once told me that the Atlantic was his front porch and the Pacific was his back deck, and that he preferred to sleep under the stars. But I happen to know that he almost never slept "under the stars." In fact I know I had once heard him complain that he didn't have his *"Bamboo Pillow,"* while camping out at a jazz fest in upstate New York.

All the same it was a cool way to live (I thought), and I knew that he spoke with experience. Whenever he spoke it was from experience. You could just see it in his eyes, as if he were in another world, reliving it again and again.

Curiously, Burt had his ideas about money, and still, while he would explain them to me he would simultaneously be instilling in me the *drive* for monetary gain, my own home, and property ownership. He would eventually unveil his motivation to me, but not before exposing me to various 'tests of character.' This, I assumed, was his way of assuring himself that I was worth his time and effort.

The more I learn now, the more I understand just how diverse of a mix between mysticism and science his visions truly were. Burt was certainly eclectic. He was clearly well read and had devised many new theories of his own. Primarily he remained sided with the more grounded thinkers throughout history to the present. Although some of his more forward thinking theories would at times seem far fetched and often left much to be explained. To which he would remind me that *my* capacity to grasp certain complexities had not yet formed. This was an understatement. I was taking in everything I could, and still I had a long way to go. There will always be much left to discover. It's in the pursuit of this knowledge that you discover your true path.

By all accounts, Burt was without doubt some type of genius. Although, it is a little difficult to place him in any specific field of study as he did appear to have a working knowledge in several. He had spoken several times of spending a few years (when he was younger) studying at Yale (unofficially). He said that he was living in New Haven (Connecticut) at the time and had a number of friends who were students at the school. After some time, continuously crashing in various friends' dorm rooms after parties and what have you, he then just began attending random lectures throughout the day. He said that he took endless notes, which amazingly he still had in his possession. These were tattered old composition notebooks, with the yellowed pages sitting loose between the covers like file folders. He kept these in plastic grocery bags that were tied up tight, with numerous bags tied up within each other. Burt had clarified for me that these were the culmination of his years at Yale, along with a handful of *other* notable institutions across the country as well. The notes rarely ever came out and I actually only saw them a couple of times.

It was common for Burt to have some snippet of information on *any* topic that would come up. It could get exhausting at times, but it did make you wonder just how and where an old man of his status had the time to acquire this amount of information. Later I would learn *how* exactly it was that he did know so much, and my quest to figure that out had turned into the pages you are reading here. If you decide to adhere to the principles throughout this story, chances are you too can attain a level of knowledge not unlike Burt's, and perhaps beyond.

Another of Burt's traits which I had taken notice of, was the fact that he was so incredibly adept with mechanics of *any* sort. It truly was alarming to find just how precise and meticulous he could be, being that his fingers resembled sausages (with knuckle hair). Oddly enough he was still able to fix very tiny things, like the insides of old watches for example and other things like that.

He was also very much devoted to his exercise. In the very early hours each morning he would rise to the moonlight to put himself through rigorous routines. Whether it was the side-step shuffles or the rigidly performed toe-touches, at times some of the 1950's exercise moves could look completely ridiculous. I half expected to see him on one of those machines with the big rubber band jiggling around the waist band area. In all fairness though, I was envious. His motivation was inspiring. It was his power *to* motivate that would draw you to him.

Buprenorphine and Methadone

In order for you to have the best possible chances for success you are going to have to find yourself a clinic and begin a regimen of medicines to aid in your transition. The powerhouse of the latest substance abuse medication line-up is buprenorphine. I used it, and anyone I know who has gotten clean had used it, or, in some cases methadone.

The methadone is not my recommendation. I was on it at one time and so were many of the acquaintances I had made over the years. It was not a pleasant experience at all. What had happened was I would keep bumping up my dose, just as most others do, until I was on enough of a dose that I would literally pass out standing up. It happened to me at the grocery store one time and it was embarrassing as hell. But these are simply *my* experiences, and so this is not to say that the methadone is a bad choice for your individual situation. A great many people have effectively changed their lives with methadone, and therefore I've got to give credit where it is due.

Methadone is a very cheap, very old medication. Which is why the insurance companies were in such favor of it at one time. German scientists had created the drug in an effort to find a more cost efficient, locally produce-able alternative to morphine. This was wartime and supplies which required components from other countries had become a serious issue the world over.

The major issue with methadone (from my experience) is the fact that many patients that are on it still get high. Typically, when you give a dirty urine while on buprenorphine, the clinic will usually warn you once and then terminate you if you do it a second or third time. However, it seemed as though the methadone clinic would tend to treat dirty urines a bit differently. Instead, when you produced a dirty sample *there*, their first response was to up your dose because, the idea is, if your continuing to get high then your current dose must not be sufficient. This often works out well for the addict who is attempting to maintain a cocaine habit, while routinely attending the clinic. One of the usual reasons being that, the higher the dose the more cocaine one can ingest before experiencing the 'come down.'

Visit a methadone clinic any morning of the week, except Sunday, and observe everything going on around you. It is often a motley crew of unkempt, pajama'd addicts, in line itching for their dose or in the parking lot making pill deals. Then, research and locate the nearest buprenorphine clinic and compare the findings as I have. Chances are you will come to a similar conclusion regarding the effectiveness comparison between the two medications, and my inclination to lean toward the bupenorphine for the best possible results.

Magnum

Although I did not want to seem nosey, it had been a couple of months now that I had been friends with Burt and I still had no idea where it was that he was staying. It had become clear that it wasn't at the shelter, but *where* it was I was ready to find out.

When Saturday came he and I met at the coffee shop as usual and sat and spoke for a bit. I had asked if he wanted to come over to *my* house sometime, and explained to him how I had just gotten a new ping pong table and needed someone to help me break it in. He agreed rather quickly, which surprised me a little as I kind of thought this was going to be a bit more difficult. He was always very selective with his time, but I would quickly learn why it was that he had jumped at the chance to play.

We wound up going straight from Starbucks to Sports Authority, where I decided to purchase a fresh pack of table tennis balls and two brand new paddles. We figured we might as well do it right and get fresh equipment, and I happened to be in a position where I could afford it at the time. I hadn't given it much thought, but as we were looking over all of the new stuff Burt began making comments that eluded to the fact that he has maybe played a game or two of ping pong before this. I myself am not really very good at all. In fact, each time that I had gotten into playing (in prison), I *would* excel eventually but I was definitely not naturally inclined toward it.

Just before heading to my house, I made sure to ask if he wanted to stop by *his* place for anything and he said that he was all set. So *that* didn't work. While, "Where do you live?" wasn't that invasive of a question to ask, he had just never offered up the info himself at times when others probably would have. It is a bit difficult to explain his demeanor when it came to subjects such as this. He was very set in his ways.

Anyhow, we got to my place and went straight to setting up. I put a pod of Donut Shop in the Keurig, I put some *Bob Marley* on the sound bar, and I got my ass handed to me on the ping pong table. What the hell? This guy went from sixty year old man to *Serena* friggin' *Williams* as soon as he got that damn paddle in his hand. It was a lot of fun though. I could not stop laughing. Once he spun his *Magnum PI* Detroit Tiger's hat around, that was it. I couldn't take him seriously. He was getting pissed off too, because I couldn't keep it together long enough to play a set. Each time we'd start, he would hunch down and begin bouncing side to side with that backwards Magnum hat, it was just too much.

One item of interest that I can remember taking notice of that night, was how Burt would never wear short sleeve shirts. This being the case, it would be some time before I had gotten another look at the tattoo. Anyway, I did finally get serious and it didn't help much because he just about shut me out several times over. He never did explain where he had developed his skills, but he was very in tune with what *I* was doing wrong and his suggestions were quite useful. After playing til the evening he had a friend come and pick him up at my house. I had remembered *after* they had left that *I* wanted to drop him off, so that I could perhaps find out where it was that he lived, though that answer would come soon enough.

Counseling & Treatment

We as addicts tend to be guarded when talking to others about our own addiction. Not to say that we don't talk about it, but we *are* prone to be somewhat choosey on who we open up to. I myself don't always feel comfortable when talking to a therapist whom I sense as having a limited *textbook* knowledge regarding addiction.

There are also some therapists who talk of their sobriety from alcohol and drugs, and yes, I do believe that they probably have smoked a few joints and cracked a few too many beers in their day, but it's just not sufficient when faced with a hardcore opiate addict. Even if they *have* attended AA ever since high school, that does not prepare them to properly and safely guide a heroin addict who has lost everything numerous times over.

Of course, each therapist is going to have different qualities and can certainly be of benefit to the right patient, assuming they identify with those whom they are helping, and those who they are helping identify with them.

Again, this is going to be a necessary step toward your success. So you might as well concede to the fact that you will *have* to get in touch with a substance abuse counselor of some sort. Luckily there are many options when it comes to therapy. When researching them, you are going to want to take notice of the initials after their last names, as this will at least give you an idea of their training and background. Whichever med clinic you attend, they are likely going to stipulate that you attend counseling and therefore why not make the most use of this. If you have state medical coverage they usually *will* cover the fees, and often times it's the insurance company that is mandating the therapy. Still yet, be sure to ask which policies the therapist *you* select accepts, as they typically will only work with certain companies.

You are going to want a therapist who you can feel at ease with. You must not hold anything back and be as brutally honest as you can. If you cannot relax and feel comfortable around the therapist you will not be able to accomplish these things and will no doubt put your sobriety in serious jeopardy. It's OK to tell them if you would like to switch counselors, just be clear on your reasoning and they will typically understand. This is a common occurrence in this and many other fields. For instance, how long would you put up with a medical doctor who had poor bedside manner and made you feel uncomfortable, unable to express your concerns or issues? Chances are you would seek treatment elsewhere ASAP and would be right in doing so.

Burt had explained to me how for most people therapy can either be a) a huge pain in the ass, or b) a life changing experience. He went on to say that it all depends on you and how committed you are in seeking a better life for yourself. "If it doesn't feel right, change it until it does." When you do find the right one, embrace it. Relax and let the professional assist you in digging through all of the bullshit of the past, to help find the *real* you

∞

We all believe to know who we are deep down, but things happen, life happens. We get lost in the day to day grind of whatever our lifestyle is at the time. Bit by bit we are molded to fit the situations we are experiencing, and, in turn becoming less and less the person who we once strove to be. The beauty of all of this is, it is *almost* all reversible. Burt found a unique way to bring this point home for me by telling me the story of a Dr. Penfield.

It's been well documented, that, in 1931 Dr. Wilder Penfield (a prominent brain surgeon) had experienced a rather peculiar incident one afternoon while performing surgery on an epileptic patient at the Montreal Neurological Institute. While in the midst of a brain surgery, Dr. Penfield opted to stimulate what's called the 'temporal lobe' of his patient, with the assistance of an electrode. When he did so, the patient burst up and began to report having seen an incredibly detailed vision of herself giving birth to her daughter (an account that had occurred many years prior). After performing further research, Dr. Penfield concluded that within the recesses of the human brain was what he described as a "permanent record of the stream of consciousness, more detailed than any man can recall by voluntary effort."

Keeping this in mind helped me to realize that somewhere in the vast networks of our minds could exist an accessible file containing all of the thoughts, feelings, and memories that had once fueled our passion for life. As we go on day by day, we end up virtually piling so much of our stress and egotism on top that it requires a bit of time and effort to sift through, selecting which thoughts and notions to discard and which to give life to. More often than not this will prove to be a rather daunting task to take on alone, and so professional assistance is strongly advised.

I do need to add however, that Dr. Penfield's work regarding memory recall was not generally accepted. Some say that his patients were possibly experiencing hallucinations induced by the stimulation. It's still fascinating to consider, and could be taken to mean that perhaps one day doctors may be able to manipulate these types of things into treatments for Alzheimer patients. Wouldn't it be fascinating if this could allow them to regain some of if not *all* of their lost memories.

My own personal experience has been positive. As I sorted out *my* life little bits at a time, I began to have these random recollections that were getting increasingly lucid each time. These were for the most part random moments of my past which would have otherwise remained in the background never to be pondered again. To me this would have been a very sad state of mind, as I cherish each and every good memory I have.

New memories are coming all the time now and I feel fortunate that I have the time to appreciate them. Whether Dr. Penfield's work was correct or not means very little here, and is interesting if nothing else. I can only tell you that since I had begun working with Burt on *my* sobriety, I have regained a great deal of memories, and for that I am grateful.

∞

Anytime I think of residential treatment (of which I have been through several) I am reminded of a particular AA meeting that I had once attended. This meeting hosted a speaker named Dwight, who, while explaining his story and getting his message across, went on to tell us of an experience he had had while visiting a local treatment center with his family (prior to committing himself to admittance). This was to be a sort of test run, to see if he was interested in checking in.

So the liaison for the center commenced to taking he and the family for a quick tour around the facility, while at the same time explaining what a client would be involved in, were he to attend the programming there. Apparently, while visiting the cafeteria they had encountered some residents who all appeared to be happy and having a good time. The family watched as these gentlemen proceeded to engage in high fives with each other, as well as with the liaison. Dwight had likened the scene to that of some kind of distorted Sunny D commercial. It really did appear to everyone though, that this *was* a fun place.

Dwight and his family wasted no time in making the decision to go ahead and get him signed up. Excited about a new start he said his goodbyes to the family and hurriedly unpacked his things. He then headed down to the cafeteria for a quick bite to eat when he ran into the gentlemen from before. Being new to the facility he wanted to introduce himself. Remembering how friendly these same guys were earlier, Dwight approached in the most upbeat manner he could muster (as he was still kind of sick from drug withdrawals), and after saying hello and announcing his name, found that all that these guys cared to talk about now that the liaison wasn't there, was how much the place *sucked* and how *miserable* everybody was there. He was crushed. Here was Dwight, "lookin' to turn over a new leaf" (as he put it), and all ready for the high fives, and instead he got left hanging in the wind. Talk about feeling awkward.

At the very least I can say that Dwight was certainly clean and sober when *I* saw him speak, so there is a good chance that the program had worked out after all.

The important thing here is that we learn from Dwight's experience. For starters, we must try to get more information on a facility before just signing on and committing to it. With access to the internet just about everywhere now this shouldn't be that difficult. Check blogs, forums, chat rooms, and review sites (there are hundreds of them). Another lesson to be learned here is that most of us don't know *what's* going to work for our individual needs, and therefore some trial and error is going to be expected.

Francis

I was at work one Wednesday morning when I had received a somewhat frantic phone call from Burt stating that he needed to be picked up at a local university library located at one of the nearby schools. He informed me that he wasn't ready *just* yet, but that he would be right about the same time that I would be getting out of work. I agreed to find him a ride and come to the rescue, and told him I would head straight there after I got out.

My younger brother drove as we circled the campus, having a bit of a hard time finding the library. The school just appeared to be a giant maze of parking lots and one way streets. When we finally did get to him I was frustrated and wanted to get the eff' outta there. He looked glad to see us and relieved to have a ride.

As we were making our way, I thought back to his phone call to me at work and then asked why it was that he had sounded as though he were in distress. He said that it was nothing, he had had an argument with a "colleague," as he put it, and was a little worked up at the time. I then inquired as to the nature of the argument and he was of course ever cryptic with his response. He said that he was in need of certain "data" pertaining to some research that he was currently involved in, and, although he knew who to acquire it *from*, he and this gentleman were not on the best of terms with each other. This individual whom he had referred to, he said, was not being forthcoming with the information by any means. After he had gone on for a few minutes it had become clear that this was something of a more personal nature, but he eventually fell into a rant, unraveling the story for me in much more detail than I was accustomed to Burt using (in regards to his personal life and history).

Burt explained that the individual who was in possession of the specific data that *he* had required, was a physics professor at the school there. Back when the two of them were younger and Burt was staying around the area, they had both fallen for the same girl. This was some woman, Edie, who was now the dean of admissions as well as the wife of the professor.

137

Apparently, she and Burt have carried on an affair for over twenty years now with the professor kept in the dark throughout. That is until recently. The way Burt now spun this tale, it sounded like the kind of stuff daytime soaps are made of.

Francis (the professor), and Burt were one time friends who actually got along really well. They would get together to philosophize and ponder over the questions of existence. Yet when the two of them had attended the same meteor shower party (back in the early 80's), they had encountered Edie, a then budding freshman who took an interest in each of them individually. She would go on to date each of them over the course of a semester.

After a while continuing on like this, she felt as though it just wasn't fair to carry on as such any longer, and so she needed to make a decision between them. While Burt was a bit of a nomad, still searching out a niche in life, Francis, who was in his third year as an undergraduate, was of a more stable nature. With this being the case, she made the reasonable choice to stay with Francis. Burt, however, was crushed. He simply refused to let it go. Though he did manage to gain her attention off and on for many years, she would return to her husband time and again.

Throughout the years the two of them would meet just to talk, but always in secret. Burt admits that he would purposely entice her into little flings, but nothing serious and Francis was none the wiser. Until just recently, when Francis had intercepted an email of a provocative nature sent *from* Edie to Burt. This brought on a big feud amongst them and now none of them were talking.

Another result of all of this, was that I was now going to find out where exactly it was that Burt was living. I then inquired as to where it was that we had to go? I did know that he lived in Springfield, I just wasn't sure what section. Like most cities, Springfield is broken down into quadrants, or "burrows." Burt directed us to State street, where we turned off somewhere by A.I.C. (American International College), then it was a couple more turns and we were there. It was a massive old house like many others in this particular area, which is known to all as Forest Park.

Burt explained to us how he rented out the basement there, which had been fitted with an entire apartment. This was complete with it's own entrance, a kitchen, a bedroom, and a living room/den for watching television and things of that nature. He asked if we wanted to come in and check it out, as I was already getting out of the car, determined to get a look a my "guru's" lair.

While there was plenty of original architecture left in the main structure of the home, everything else had been modernized and refitted. Someone had dumped a ton of money into renovations, because the craftsmanship was absolutely immaculate. Inside there were art pieces scattered about, beautifully framed replicas on the walls, and a state of the art recording booth. This was something which both Burt and the owner would share the use of, as well as collaborate on (what Burt had called) "projects." Burt dabbled with the ukelele and the piano, while Jerry, the owner, was an avid guitarist who actually had a whole band of his own. Jerry owned his own pub downtown, and his band would perform there periodically. According to Burt they were very good, but I never did get to catch a show.

Anyhow, Burt opens a door on the back wall to reveal a rather sizable "game room" with an official league endorsed regulation table tennis table, with professional paddles, plenty of room, and comfortable chairs with little end tables between them for onlookers to relax in style. He asked if I was up for a game and I couldn't resist. I ran out to the car to get a backpack that I had carried with me for work (to keep my sneakers in). At that time I was still dressed for work with big boots on, that clearly weren't a *practical* choice for ping pong.

Burt beat up on me in ping pong for a while, until I had gotten tired and noticed that my brother was getting anxious to leave. So we decided it was just about time to call it a day and head home. Burt and I had made some quick plans to meet up as usual and we left, unknowingly leaving my backpack behind in the process. Though it did take a while, I would get my backpack back in a rather unusual fashion.

Relapse

When you first get clean and have begun to bounce back physically and mentally, one of your first instincts will be to share your good decisions with those who you are close to. It's OK, this is a good thing. However, as you may have experienced in the past, sometimes one finds that they have jumped the gun and perhaps spoke too soon.

I would have this type of thing happen to me personally, time and time again. So during my final attempt at sobriety, I began to look inside myself and really try to understand what was happening each time I would go through this.

What I had found, is that when we as addicts reveal to others of our successes, others who have been waiting (often times) years to hear such things, we tend to feel as though we've accomplished something great. You very possibly may even experience a *natural* high from the joy that this good news brings to those whom you are close to. This too is OK, because it *is* great to be free of the madness. Although, if we go and enter ourselves into this kind of situation *too* soon, our inner addict could still have enough of a grip to immediately create within us a certain sense of complacency, and thus thoughts of sneaking in just *one* bag (or whatever it is that triggers you).

With regards to announcing your sobriety, my advice would be to put it off as long as possible. Each day that passes sober, each accomplishment you achieve along the way, is all going to be more the sweeter when you do make your new life known.

One relapse prevention trick that Burt had taught me was a two-part lesson of which I was not to learn all at once. I was instructed to set my racing mind at ease, as I experienced the depression and temptation (white knuckling) during the early stages of abstinence, by assuring myself that I was not necessarily stopping all opiate use forever. However, a significant amount of sober time becomes necessary if for nothing else but one's health. Then, after a fair length of clean time has been achieved and some predetermined goals have been met, the individual shall reassess his or her particular situation. It is then that the individual reconsiders any designs on interrupting continued sobriety. This is what the first part of the lesson was, and as Burt had done with me, I will not get to the second part until (in this case) later on in the text. However, it is **paramount** that you wait until you are schooled on the second part before taking any further action.

Burt had some ideas about relapse that didn't exactly mesh with the approaches *I* had learned about while attending the programs I had been in over the years. At first I was apprehensive about committing myself to something that goes against all previous advice. However, after some careful consideration it occurred to me that I had *already* made a commitment to do whatever it took to stop my drug using, as well as succeed in life. I can now say with certainty that I am glad I did. There was something about the way in which Burt presented his ideas that would just give me this feeling of endless possibility, and I had made the decision to follow his suggestions wherever they led me. That is until they steered me wrong, only this never happened.

One more suggestion that I had later learned to be effective, was in regards to 'sober dates.' We've all either heard them or used them, but this time we go a different route with it. The plan here is to *not* put so much emphasis on the date on which you got clean. This creates a situation where, should you relapse, instead of nipping the problem in the bud and moving on, you could get really down on yourself for throwing away all of those "162 days" or whatever it is, and perhaps become vulnerable to your old ways. These are but numbers meant merely for *others'* ears, and mustn't become a 'lynch pin' for your entire program. Your recovery is expressed through your accomplishments and your ability to impact others around you in a positive manner.

If it is dealt with immediately, a relapse does *not* require one to 'start all over again' (the thought of this would be overwhelming to anyone). Let me say that again, a relapse does **not** mean an individual must start over. It does, however, mean a good weeks worth of horribly miserable days. Take it from me, I have experimented with this to the point of exhaustion and I can assure you that no matter how small of an amount one ingests, the sub conscience will *always* convince them that they are dope sick the following day. The buprenorphine will not be an option just yet, as the individual would then have an opiate in their system and most forms of 'bupe' contain a small amount of naloxone (which is an opiate antagonist). The naloxone in the buprenorphine would then attack the drug in the bloodstream, thereby forcing the individual into severe withdraw.

Relapse *is* an important part of the process. However, it is not necessary and can only be of any importance if it is responded to quickly and properly.

Moderately Recreational & Stress Free

Moderation is a concept that will take place in everything you do, now and for the rest of your life. For if you wish to remain a healthy, sober, and productive member of society, then you must learn to take *everything* in moderation. Not only the things you once perceived to be harmful habits, but habits of every sort.

Even working at one's sobriety can be an unhealthy habit if done to excess. You might say to yourself, "How could my being diligent toward my recovery be harmful to me?" Well that is simple, if it is causing you to neglect other important areas of your life, then it can be detrimental to your overall success. Believe it or not, even recreation should be thought of as an important component in maintaining your sobriety.

I myself have some hobbies that I've enjoyed for years, like playing the guitar and listening to music. Then I have others that I had found once I decided to turn my life around, like reading and educating myself. It is not difficult to choose a hobby, just find something that makes you happy and relieves you of the stress of the day. It is within this stress that our triggers do some of their most effective work, and so by finding a way to limit the amount of stress experienced or a proper outlet to manage it, we thereby limit our individual triggers' effectiveness.

∞

There will always be stresses of the day, sober or not. It's the difference between the amount of stress and the type of stress that set apart the addict lifestyle from that of the sober one. There is healthy stress and there is unhealthy stress, and the addict lifestyle drags with it an exorbitant amount of the latter.

We all must learn that those days are behind us now. Those days filled with uncertainty and gloom and doom, are all now part of what we can think of as the former self. By adhering to some basic concepts you will in turn learn how to separate your new self *from* your former self. This is much easier said than done. Many of those around you, especially relationship partners, are going to resist the new you. Even when everyone is well aware that you are doing the right thing. People seem to do this subconsciously and would never want to admit to it.

What I have learned is this: Because the accepted attitude toward your recovery is supposed to be a positive and supportive one, then those who are close to you are going to feel as though, since they are in support of and would do anything to aid in getting you better, that they are martyrs for your cause. However, in all likelihood many will buck your efforts to change without even knowing it. People generally do not like change, good or bad. Here you are changing at such a drastic rate that others begin to develop this unique type of inferiority complex. Sometimes others will display signs that would suggest they believe you are trying to, in some way, outdo them with your hard work and diligence.

You mustn't let yourself get sucked into this kind of 'whirlwind' of nonsense. It could quickly turn into something far worse than if you had just let it be. Your best bet here is to take it all with a grain of salt. We are all humans capable of making mistakes and therefore we must learn to live and let live. It isn't that these people want you to fail, quite the opposite I'm certain of it. They just want you to be safe and sober without disrupting *their* lives too much. This is understandable, *they* didn't ruin your life you did. Now you are making more waves by taking on a completely *different* lifestyle and perhaps inadvertently imposing it upon them.

Trust and believe that this is all typical behavior and should not be dwelled upon. Change is difficult for everyone, for if it weren't we would not be in this predicament.

If there ever were a group of people who should understand the power of forgiveness, it is addicts. We have each been granted forgiveness as individuals countless times. When working to achieve one's goals, there will be many situations where your forgiveness is in order, and so it is in your

146

best interest to get used to this concept. We do not always recognize when it is on us to do the forgiving, and so therefore it is necessary to keep a watch out for moments such as these.

Albany

Each time I thought I was beginning to get a good read on Burt, he would hit me from deep left field with some kind of 'secret to life' or another foreign language that I had no idea he was fluent in, and there were at least a few. To me, that was amazing in itself. I had spent years attempting to learn Spanish, as I wanted to be able to say I took something with me from all that time I had spent in prison and on the block chillin' with my Latino friends. While I *can* follow some conversations, I still have a hard time with sentence structure any time I attempt to join in.

It was a Thursday when Burt and I had met up at the coffee shop as usual. Before I was able to take a seat, Burt instructed me not to bother and said that I should come outside with him, he had something that he wanted to show me. So after I ordered and received my coffee he and I walked out of Starbuck's and around to the back parking lot.

As we came upon this very glitzy sports coupe parked at an angle (to protect it from dings), Burt said "What do you think, not bad huh?"

There wasn't any other car nearer to us than this, so it was clear he was referring to the Lexus that was in front of us. Before I could begin to comment on the beauty of the car, or ask where it had even come from, Burt sort of cuts me off and then launches into a rant about other people parking so close to him. He informed me that this car had belonged to a 'friend' and that he was just borrowing it for a couple of days. He then insists that we must stop by *my* house to grab some things, we were going on a trip. He explained that he had arranged this trip to be taken over the course of that day and the next, so as not to affect my work schedule. Burt said that the trip could be beneficial for me in the long run, but I couldn't get him to elaborate on that. Still, I trusted him completely and I *was* curious, so I went along with it.

∞

The car was beautiful, it was a Lexus GS250, with all leather interior and power everything. It had little TV screens scattered throughout, with a DVD player and a PlayStation connected to them. I wasn't all that acquainted with vehicles of this caliber and it certainly felt cushy riding in it. I honestly didn't even think that Burt had a driver's license before that, but it had just never come up.

After stopping home for some clothes, we hit the highway like a rocket. Burt had his plan well thought out and he was on his way. There would be no stopping him at this point.

This is how he was, quick and decisive. He was always on point, and could make some people feel uncomfortable at times when exercising his wit. He had no qualms about putting *certain* people on the spot and testing their limits. It could be amusing at times, *especially* when it was directed at someone who may have been conveying a bit of a 'know-it-all' attitude. He would usually catch them off-guard, which would result in a stutter, then a red face, followed by a change of topic, but that wouldn't usually fly with Burt. However, he clearly had a conscience about this because anytime he would bump heads with someone in this way, he would then spend the rest of the time trying to make up for it.

∞

We've reached a portion of the story here where things become somewhat complicated, and therefore I ask that you proceed with an open mind and the realization that, whether or not you *agree* with the words you are reading is of little importance, rather you understand their meaning and the reasoning for which they have been included here.

After about 45 minutes on the highway, Burt put the blinker on (this was one that made extra loud clicking sounds) and took the exit ramp into Worcester Massachusetts. We got off and stopped at a bank so that he could use the ATM. I had never seen him use an ATM before, and so I was kind of curious. As I was watching him struggle to figure out the right buttons to push, I offered my assistance.

"Whatever, if you think you can work this thing then go for it!" he barked back, appearing quite aggravated.

So I took his card and asked how much I was supposed to get out for him.

Burt proceeded to tell me that he needed to withdraw $5,000 from his savings account, and he wanted me to take it out at this ATM. By this point I'm full of questions, because none of this is making any sense. I didn't even know that he had *any* money, and how is it that he thinks an ATM is going to give him that much loot? And above all that, why so much?

Not to mention, I was beginning to wonder where it was that we were even going? Well, after some back and forth nonsense about the inner workings of ATM machines, he explained to me that this was actually *his* bank. This made it possible, once I explained things to him, to go inside and withdraw the money, and so that is what he did. And I, was taken aback. All this time I had been under the impression that the guy was completely broke, and now this, it just seemed bizarre. This was a reoccurring theme with him though, to let me ponder things for a while before coming clean with the full story. While I knew there was probably *some* reason for this, it could certainly be frustrating.

As we got back on the highway I began with my torrent of questions, to which Burt requested that I relax and listen as he tells me the story about a role model which he himself had become consumed with thirty years ago, Sir Isaac Newton. Of course I obliged, and he then went on to enlighten me of the well known, and not so well known pursuits that Newton had partaken in. Through research, I have pieced the information back together here as best as

I could.

He began to explain how we as a society would not be where we were today, as far as technology is concerned, were it not for Newton and his realization that the laws of gravity apply in space, as they do here on earth. *As above, so below.* Burt was obsessed with Newton, as well as with the topic of alchemy. In alchemy, one common theme is: "As above, so below," and so this is essentially what Newton had explained using science and mathematics. After learning of this, it's interesting to find out that Newton was also famously known to be a diligent occultist, searching deep into alchemy for the answers to the questions of the universe.

Burt had stated to me in confidence, that he had, through years of experimentation, devised a theory pertaining to the possibility of creating a *certain* form of the 'Philosopher's Stone,' through introducing an individual to various methods of intellectual, physical, and spiritual stimulation, with the objective of assisting one in achieving an enlightened conscience. The search for a way to transmutate metals using a form of this Philosopher's Stone, I learned, is a pursuit that had been taken up by alchemists the world over for many centuries. Although *Burt's* experiment was not one that would transmutate metals, but instead did something far more important, which he explained, was the very essence of the process he had been attempting to walk *me* through.

By researching the subjects of addiction, substance abuse treatments, recovery, mental health, et al., he was then able to understand just where it was that these other formulas had been attending to ineffectively. He made the decision many years ago to unite this devastating disease with an ancient science (alchemy) of which he had considerable knowledge. Burt said that he had been attending lectures and studying research regarding *both* subjects for many years now, and, faced with the mountain of data that he had accumulated, he felt he was ready to now put his thoughts into action. However, he first needed to find a subject who fell under a specific set of parameters. Someone like myself for instance, who had been through the ringer, was recently sober, and open to fresh ideas.

Burt said that each man has within him the capacity to achieve a higher level of consciousness, yet we don't all know that we want to, nor would we know how to go about it. Although, if we did, imagine for a minute a world where all men and women were of an enlightened state, in tune with the universe, and in control of their own destiny. Consider the accomplishments that humans have achieved thus far, and the fact that this has been made possible with the efforts of a mere fraction of our population. What if *every* man and woman on earth were aware of their place in life, and had a firm grasp on the way our universe worked? The possibilities would be unthinkable.

If you don't already know, or perhaps just don't remember a whole lot about Isaac Newton, then it's worth reminding you first of all that he was father to the Laws of Gravity. He had also created a brand new form of math called calculus, which, were it not *for* this math, we could not have reached the moon, predicted weather patterns, or analyzed the stock market, among thousands of other uses.

Newton was obsessed with religion *and* science, and openly professed the two inherently linked, at a time when making such claims could land him in either prison, or a far worse place, such as the gallows.

He had owned (somewhere in the range of) two hundred and fifty bibles, which he had kept held in his own library (with some sixteen hundred volumes in it), and wrote more on theology (and alchemy), than math and science combined. Still yet, he never published any non-scientific or non-mathematical writings. In fact, it wasn't until the 1930's that the world had learned *of* this mysterious side to Newton, finding more than one hundred and twenty-five manuscripts which he had written on the topic of alchemy, but never published. This information was largely ignored by the scientific community, and has only recently become taught as a subject all its own.

Could you really blame Sir Isaac though? Alchemy was outlawed at that time, as the crown had feared their currency would be tainted, riddled with counterfeit gold created by phony or conniving alchemists looking for a get rich quick scheme. Not to mention the troubles that those who had come before him had had, like Galileo for instance, who was jailed for opposing the standard belief held at *that* time, that the sun rotated around the earth.

Newton firmly believed that Jesus *was* the son of God, but that He was not *equal* to God, and therefore opposed the Holy Trinity (Father, Son, and the Holy Spirit). He claimed it was blasphemy to worship Jesus equally as you would God. This would not go over well with the crown at all, and he was, for a time, thought of as a "crazy" person, resorting to seclusion and digging deeper and deeper into his occult experimentation. Although, it was Newton's time *during* seclusion, as well as his meetings with such great minds as Edmond Halley (of the same name we associate with the comet), that had enabled him to produce what's referred to now as the 'most important mathematical text ever written.'

Newton would soon release his grand theory, which was titled "Philosophae Naturalis Principia Mathematica," more commonly known as "The Principia." This highly intricate piece of literature would go on to take the world by storm. It consisted of three books which were written in Latin, and were released July 5 1687. Most people at that time could not understand it, but knew there was definitely something to it. Many of the calculations performed through it are still used today, and are profoundly important in each of our daily lives.

So anyhow, Burt had this plan, and it pertained to me, you, and pretty much all of us. He saw a better world ahead, which, if you were to poll the country, you would find that right now many are foreseeing the complete opposite. With that in mind, it could be inspiring to hear at least *someone* talk of a better future, as opposed to all of the gloom and doom that many seem to be preaching these days.

I had soon learned that this is what he had been working on over the past thirty years of his life.

Alchemy has been with us since what *many* believe to be the beginning of humanity. As a result of this, the desire to find the truth has led to more archeologists finding the facts to confirm that this is true. It began as a search for a better connection to God, and was performed by many of history's brightest minds spanning the globe. Many were on a quest to satisfy materialistic goals by searching for the coveted 'Philosopher's Stone,' which was said to take the form of a red powder. This red powder was derived from several different compounds, which were then smelted down and subsequently put through various symbolic steps. The result was said to be a substance that contained the power to aid one in transmutating lesser based metals, like lead for instance, into the much sought after raw gold bullion, in addition to some other interesting effects.

While the transmutation of metals was only one of the stone's abilities, it was definitely the most practiced. However, many alchemists also sought to bring about *other* abilities the stone was said to have, which included, immortality, and the potential to aid in the spirits "evolution from a state of imperfection and vice, to that of a higher state of enlightenment...the purification and rejuvenation of the body."

Burt had told of the way in which this idea had consumed him for years. He experimented (over time) with many of the "secret" practices that the subject of alchemy contained, and when researching the topic myself I had learned that there are hundreds if not thousands of them. If you decide to research the topic of alchemy for *yourself*, you will quickly learn that it takes a certain type of mind to attempt to even read these ancient manuals, let alone practice the methods held within them. Do not be discouraged however, as I am told it is through consistent effort that we begin to comprehend bits and pieces at a time. Still, at first much of it *can* appear to be a collection of purposely confusing terms, sparsed throughout mystical, hard to interpret practices. Which it is, sort of.

Understand that most writings on the matter are from hundreds of years ago, when people spoke in way unlike that of today. When they had made efforts to disguise and encrypt the information for purposes such as keeping the practices sacred, or disallowing dangerous tools into the hands of 'unfavorables,' they undoubtedly vaulted the material even further by using very specific dialects and perhaps more locally used phrases. All of this makes for the majority of the quality material that is out there on the subject, to be riddled with terminologies that are generally unknown by the typical layman.

Burt went on to tell me how there were seven stages to the alchemical transmutation process that *he* was interested in, the Emerald Formula. This formula, or method, was attributed to Hermes, who is represented by the planet Mercury. The Emerald Formula is based on the inscribings on an emerald stone tablet that was said to hold 'The Secret of the Universe' or 'Blueprint of Creation.' The tablet was reportedly on display at one time in Egypt, but had long since gone missing. Each stage was said to hold within it the power to influence various aspects of our world.

Take for instance the first step, calcination, which is represented by the astrological sign Aries. It is said to hold within it the ability to influence our egos, as well as our attachment to material possessions. Quoted as being, "a naturally humbling process," it is said to ignite the fire of introspection and self-evaluation, helping to tune the body, and to burn off the excesses of over indulgence. It is also said to be represented by the revolutionaries of time who were bent on over throwing the status quo.

Clearly these are some bold claims alone, and this is just the first stage. Coincidentally, they ring true of all key issues that an individual with an addiction problem would want to address. However, I am not qualified to explain alchemy in the proper detail it requires, and so therefore this is something that you *should* take on for yourself. With that being said, should you decide to look further into the topic, I would advise taking a course aimed at helping you to translate the ancient literature available. There are a few courses that I know of, and if you Google the topic they're easy to find.

While watching an instructional video aimed at enhancing one's capacity to understand alchemy, I had learned of some interesting facts. One, for example, had caught my attention when considering all of the alchemical references made in main stream media, which was something that Burt had only recently opened my eyes to. Anyhow, I had learned that Gene Roddenberry, creator and head writer for the original *Star Trek* series as well as *Star Trek: The Next Generation,* was actually a master alchemist in addition to being a master magician. It's interesting to go back and watch these shows after taking an interest in the topic of alchemy, and then subsequently being able to spot some of the references made throughout both.

In order to learn the teachings of alchemy, we must first learn to structure our thought process. It is only then, once you have attained the ability to take notice, that you will begin to see how our society, is, and always has been, heavily influenced by the alchemical world. There are alchemical influences found in almost every facet of our lives, including: our currency, our language, our political structures, our entertainment, and above all, the Bible. In fact, it is said that with the right guidance and knowledge, one can use the teachings of alchemy to 'unlock' the Bible and have it virtually "open up and blossom like a flower," as one master alchemist put it.

The language of alchemy is spoken throughout the world in an ever expanding list of ways. It is the objective of the alchemical student, after studying the material, to acquire the rigidity and discipline necessary to observe the world around them, and, in effect be able to understand when an alchemical reference is being made and the reason why it *has* been made.

All of this brings about the need to discuss another one of Burt's 'life hacks.' He had assured me that many who are interested in these topics and decide to make an attempt at studying them, may find that they have a hard time adjusting their thought process, unable to completely give their thoughts and feelings to the subject matter. He explained that this was a state of mind which he had dubbed "stuck." Citing that the 'cogs of the brain' were simply "in a bind" and could easily be freed up with the proper "tool," he then explained that, after experimenting with various mediums, *he* had found to be *crosswords.* Huh? Is along the lines of whatever it was that I must have said at the time. That is until I had discovered that it does in fact work *quite* well when the individual makes a sufficient effort with it.

What happens is an all too common scenario. We as individuals get overwhelmed with the stress of our daily lives, letting this consume us and leaving very little energy left for the brain to operate. Sure, we feel on point and perhaps function at a normal pace, but once we try to shift gears and take on a new direction, we find that our brains are not conditioned for the task and hence another failed attempt results.

So for this, Burt said, crosswords are precisely the right tool for the job. If you have never done them before, your going to want to start with the really easy ones. Yet before you do that, take a look at some of the difficult puzzles, he explained, and see if you can fill in *any* of the answers. The typical response would be no or perhaps a couple at best. The idea that he wants you to understand is that once you fully allow yourself to give thought to the puzzles and learn the inner workings involved, you should develop the capacity to complete them quickly, at a difficulty level beyond that which you had once perceived to be possible.

As you begin to work your way through these puzzles, tiny jolts are sent throughout various regions of the brain not typically used, awakening these areas and effectively getting your brain 'in shape.' Once you reach the more difficult levels you will also find that there are going to be numerous terms and facts that you had no idea you even knew about, all of which causing your thought patterns to shift gears while conditioning your brain in the process. Be sure to pick up a quality dictionary and thesaurus, as these will become key tools when learning how to solve *any* crossword puzzles. Burt recommends that you spend a few weeks working on them, while upping your time spent reading as well.

It was strongly suggested by Burt that we continue reading as much as possible. Reading, he explained, will eventually provide the answers you seek, as long as you remain focused and stay on track. He assures us that the knowledge required to effectively make a lasting change in our lives will almost always come from an unexpected source. It is for this reason that he recommends you consume yourself with a vast variety of topics. As people who have not been very connected with ourselves for some time now, we as addicts do not know *what* it is that will inspire our motivation to grab for something better, and so it is through experimenting with a wide selection of topics that we are to seek this.

When I first began to take literature seriously, it wasn't in school unfortunately, but during my third or fourth prison experience. At that time I had this cellmate who happened to be familiar with the medication that the prison had me on. It wasn't a narcotic, but it apparently still held a value (or so I would find out). He had inquired as to whether or not I was interested in selling them to him, and I had doubts about the whole idea at the start. He would bring up the question a number of times, and said that he would give me whatever I wanted for them. I did eventually give in and had decided that I would try and see what it was that I could get out of it.

What I would do is, each day when the 'med cart' would come around to the cell block, I would have to engage in a bit of deception in order to cheek my meds (the med-techs would always be looking for this), give them to my roommate, and he in return would have his mom mail me brand new books from Amazon. I can't say that I am proud of this of course, but at this time I had yet to be rescued from this disease and was still of a very different frame of mind. Anyway, this roommate said that I could select any books that I chose, and so in an effort to begin with a solid foundation I had opted to go with some of the classics. You know, those books that they probably wanted me to read in school but I unfortunately never had, like *Animal Farm* by George Orwell, *Catcher in the Rye* by JD Salinger, or *One Flew Over the Cuckoos Nest* by Ken Kesey, for example.

I had become obsessed, for a time, with books that were generally known to make use of metaphors, with the objective of conveying a political or spiritual message. I thought this was a fascinating use of the English language, and by my searching for more interesting examples I had been exposed to a fair amount of classic literature. Coincidentally, the very act of working my way through more and more of the material had helped to bring light to a number of forgotten 'life lessons,' many of which I had just about abandoned.

Were it not *for* books of this nature, I would probably never have read as much fiction as I had. It was my new found interest in *certain* fictional works that had led me to read some selections from Dan Brown. Brown is a prominent best selling author who has written many books, such as *The Divinci Code* and *Angels and Demons*. These, as well as the majority of Brown's novels, are packed full of factual information pertaining to topics such as esoterism, American history, the occult, and religion. Brown, who is a modern literary giant, wraps the information neatly inside some fast paced, page turning fictional novels, a couple of which went on to become extremely successful full scale motion pictures.

I wanted to be sure myself, and I urge you as well, to approach books and topics of this nature with an open mind, while at the same time a cautious one. I say this, simply because you are at a vulnerable stage in your life right now and are susceptible to being swayed in one unforeseeable direction or another. With that being said, some of these texts can contain some rather 'off the wall' ideals, and should be defined with an unbiased attitude. I stress this in an effort to avoid a situation where you are subscribing to certain mindsets without first developing a clear picture of the message and the objective behind the text.

∞

As we were reaching Albany New York it was abut 5 O'clock in the afternoon. We were arriving just in time to catch the rush hour traffic on the highway, which had us at a dead stop for about twenty minutes or so. I began to let my mind wander as I stared at the chugs of factory smoke billowing out over the city and revealing signs of industrious life ahead. I recall this sight causing me to think back to when *Springfield* had once chugged like this, and how, thankfully, it seems that we may just now be on the rise to success once again. With a new casino opening downtown, in addition to the marijuana dispensaries that will be coming soon (Massachusetts had legalized recreational use), and it is clear to see that this is going to be a whole new world for us. The city had been fighting a downward slump for many years, and we're just now finally bouncing back.

I was beginning to get hungry, to which Burt had asked that I hold out just a little longer. He informed me that he was on a strict time schedule, but assured me that if I just be patient he had already made plans for us regarding food. I conceded, as usual, and then began to eat some *Chuckle's* that I had found in the center console. Burt said they weren't his, but to go for it, still not offering any info on whose car this actually *was*.

I remember thinking about the money that Burt had taken out at the bank, and decided that I didn't see any harm in asking him about it.

"Just out of curiosity Burt, what *is* all that cash about anyway?" I inquired, as humbly as I could manage.

"I'm not sure yet, ask me again tomorrow" he replied, while appearing to be in deep thought. Although he *may* have just been acting as such, in an effort to keep me from inquiring any further. At any rate, this was all I could get Burt to say about the matter, and so I had made a mental note to hold him to that same question the following day.

It wasn't long after the *Chuckles* that we were exiting the pike and taking the 787 into downtown Albany. I believe it was the Broadway street exit for those who are familiar with the city. Albany in my opinion is a really fun town to visit, though I *am* somewhat bias. My first experience with the city was back in 1993, and it was to attend the first Grateful Dead concert that I had ever gone to. This one night of live music, hallucinogenic drugs, and hordes of interesting people, would go on to become the catalyst for the time I had spent on the road after that, and is more than likely the reasoning behind my affection for the city. Back then the Knickerbocker (Albany's civic center) was called the Pepsi Arena, and was still, after seeing the Dead play all around the country, one of my favorite arenas to catch a show.

As we approached North Pearl street I could see that Burt had turned the signal on once again, and I recall I had gotten a tad anxious, as I *was* well acquainted with the area. You see, back when the Dead did come to town, any town, their fans would swarm onto the city like locusts, increasing in number as the showtime would near. These fans would, traditionally, show up very early, sometimes the day before and some the week before.

They would first select a location, one that was in the vicinity of the venue's main entrance, and then proceed to setting up their wares. These little mobile "kiosks" (using the term broadly here) usually consisted of a collection of random items, like shirts, jewelry, food, etc. In addition to those, there were also venders of another sort (unfortunately), ones who offered *certain* products, that, while they weren't legal, were even more profitable (drugs). The area that *all* of these things took place, was, and is known by many as "Shakedown Street." Borrowing from a title of one of the Dead's many songs, if listened to, one can see that the lyrics essentially explain what a Shakedown Street actually *is*. This area that we were currently entering was where I had first experienced those memories about twenty-five years before.

Anyhow, I soon heard Burt's blinker come clicking on yet once more, and this time it would be for a destination. It had to be. The only possible turns that he could make now were either a hotel or an empty lot. We pulled into the Hilton Hotel and it was then that I actually got some information out of Burt. He explained that we had reservations for the night here, separate rooms (all paid for), as well as dinner seats waiting at the hotel restaurant for whatever we wanted to eat. Burt said that with all that this hotel had to offer, as well as the downtown area there, should be plenty enough to occupy us for the night. He explained that we were going to see some friends of his the following morning. This was enough to change *my* spirits, for now anyway (I mean come on, this is the Hilton).

I was psyched, and wasn't really accustomed to this kind of treatment. There was complimentary everything, an activity guide, a huge flat screen TV, video games, a full gym, and a fully stocked mini-bar with an impressive selection of snacks and beverages. Though it was apparent that Burt had phoned ahead prior and asked that there be no liquor available in the room. This, I learned due to a card that the staff had left on the coffee table. While this *was* meant to be a gesture for my sake, I had never been a fan of alcohol *anyhow*. Though I did appreciate the thought.

It had been a couple of hours now and I had reached a point where I felt I deserved some answers. I wasn't going to wait any longer and so I took to making my stand.

"Alright Burt, enough's enough, what the hell's goin' on here?" I demanded, in a sort of lighthearted manner.

"You wouldn't believe me if I told you" he snapped right back, as if he were anticipating my inquiry.

Bullshit, he knew damn well I'd believe him. But this was an evasive measure, one that I had come to expect. I had also known that any more energy put into this was going to be a wasted effort, and so I chose to drop it once again.

We went and had a nice sit down meal at the hotel restaurant. I had the sliders, each with lots of bacon (or as much as you can fit on them), along with some home fries. Burt got a ceaser's salad with a side order of banana split. Did I mention he loved ice cream? Burt looooved ice cream. I mean, I'm a fan as well, but he took it to a whole other level.

Now these, I'm sure, do not sound like sit down entrees to you, but we had just never given a *damn* about things like that. Anyway, as we're sitting there, I began to wonder if Burt had been to this hotel before, as the desk clerk and the waiter have now *each* addressed him in a fashion that would suggest so. I then noticed the waiter holding up a bottle of wine and heading our way with it, as if Burt had an ongoing routine of some kind and they're just going ahead as they normally would. Well, Burt raised his arm and back the waiter went. It was after that that I was certain that there was definitely more going on with Burt than I maybe had realized, but I couldn't get a read on *what*.

"You know Burt, you don't need to abstain from alcohol on my account. Really, the gesture alone is enough," I explained.

"Is that what you think kid?" he called me kid a lot. "I'm not doin' it for you so much as I am myself," he gruffed, "I'm just sayin', I've resorted to cuttin' back these days is all."

And I couldn't be certain, but I began to suspect shenanigans. In other words a fib, a lie, an heir of untruth in his tone, mischief afoot.

After dinner, we walked around the city for a little while, checking out the 'sights.' Burt suggested that we go and see a movie, which is when I had begun to give him a hard time and ask if we were "on a date now or what?" He said that he noticed a theater nearby and figured it sounded like a good enough idea. I agreed, and so we went and saw the only thing that was starting soon, "The Conjuring."

Ten minutes into the film Burt had gotten up to go "use the phone," and was gone for over 45 minutes. I went looking for him in the bathroom and out by the entrance, but he was nowhere to be found. So I returned to my seat and continued to watch the film. When he finally did come back, he seemed to be winded. I asked him what took so long, and he said that he had just gotten tied up on the phone with a friend whom he hadn't talked to in quite a while.

I was exhausted by the time the movie was over. It had just been such a long day that my mind and body both needed rest. Burt agreed and we returned to the hotel, said goodnight and that was it. Still no explanation for why we were even here, but I had figured since I had my own room all paid for, to heck with it, tomorrow is another day.

I awoke to Burt banging on my door. It was 5:30 in the morning and I had just gotten to sleep a couple hours before. I opened the door to find him standing there, all dressed and ready for the day with his jacket on.

"Mornin'," he said, "you gonna let me in or what?" As I'm stepping aside wondering what *this* was all about.

"Hey it's chilly out there this morning, make sure you wear a sweater," he informs me in a tone that was meant to motivate.

"I don't own *sweaters* Burt, why, you've been outside already?" Remembering how he wakes up for exercise everyday, I answered my own question. *Those damn shuffles.*

He explained to me that we were checking out, grabbing some breakfast on the move and meeting up with some local friends of his. He was suspiciously quiet this particular morning, where usually he was ranting on about one thing or another. I wondered if there was trouble with whatever it was that he had brought us here for.

After a quick breakfast at some greasy spoon on the corner, we drove a few blocks down to an apartment complex, stopped in front and Burt tooted the horn a couple taps. I jumped out and got in the back seat so that Burt's friend could have shotgun. It was only a second or two before the apartment door swung open, and I kid you not, a real life effin' clown came bursting out. Now I wasn't sure what to make of this, but he *ran* to the car, jumping in with no hesitation and Burt then sped off without a word.

This guy turned around to look at me, and I just gave this sort of half-hearted wave and said "Hey there, how ya' doin'?" He was a nice old clown though, who introduced himself to me as Larry the Clown, or "just Larry" would be fine. He had a giant lipstick smile painted on, with a Ronald McDonald type of wig, and Shaquille O'Neal sized sneakers. You could tell it wasn't clown make-up, per se, but more like a hastily put together collage of his wife's cosmetics. Also, instead of the typical giant clown shoes, his were some really big Converse All-Stars that he had stuffed something into the toes of. He was a pleasant enough guy though, and from the sound of things he and Burt had been pals for a long time. The two of them carried on together, laughing, remembering old times, and bickering over mundane details and dates. Now this scene would have been unremarkable, were it not for the fact that the guy was in a wig and lipstick, while smoking a Newport and swearing like a late night comedian.

They took a minute to explain to me how we were now on our way to a nearby hospital. They told me how Larry makes the trip down there himself once a week and puts on a show for the children who permanently live there, and that he usually has a helper for his props and whatnot (there was a storage room at the hospital filled with toys and things). Only, the person who would normally be there to help out could not make it this time, and so therefore Burt and I were just along to assist him. It sounded positive at the least, which *was* another trait of Burt's, to keep things positive.

We had arrived at the hospital fairly quick. While jumping out of the car I had noticed Burt taking the fanny pack that held the five grand, out of the trunk, for, what I thought was the first time he had touched it since he put it there. I had always hated those fanny packs, I just always thought they looked completely ridiculous. That *was* Burt's style sometimes though, ridiculous.

By the time we had gotten inside and on the ward it was around 8 am. It was clear right away that Larry's arrival was well received. All of the kids on this ward were cancer patients, who, sadly, were in a terminal stage. A visit from Larry may be the highlight of the week for some of these kids and it really made you think, to visit them face to face, mortality suddenly seemed so fragile and unappreciated.

You tend to think about the ways in which you've abused your own body, and how you have taken it for granted. You also think about your loved ones. You think about how you would respond if this ever happened to one of them, and how you would want to do whatever was possible to ease their pain and take away the stress. You also wonder how it is you could have wasted so much precious time.

While watching Larry do his thing, kids are laughing and climbing out of their beds. The nurse is running this way telling one child to get back into bed, then that way complaining of socks being thrown around the room, which was all kind of comical from a distance. Amongst the fracas, I caught sight of Burt standing in the hallway with one of the older doctors, whom he had previously pointed out to me and said was a friend of his, Dr. Rosenberg.

I watched as the doctor handed Burt a file folder (that was chock full of paperwork) and they then shook hands, only, not in the way in which one shakes with a stranger, but with each one grasping the other man's wrist (or forearm area). That definitely looked weird. And in an interesting addition to things, when we made it back to the car and Burt was throwing his fanny pack in the trunk, oddly, it was now empty but for what could only have been a few bills.

We dropped Larry back at his apartment, said goodbye and hit the highway, back on our way home. Burt asked that I drive and told me not to worry about my having a suspended license, he would handle any problems should they arise. I'm not sure what it is he thought he would be able to do, but it would just be one of thousands of times that I had driven unlicensed anyhow, so I agreed. Burt pulled over, we did the "Chinese fire drill" (as he called it), and we were off again. I would bust his stones about this phrase possibly being construed as racist, which was perhaps the only way I had *ever* found to ruffle *his* feathers.

As I drove, *cautiously*, Burt sat in the passenger seat rifling through the pile of documents that the file from the doctor had contained. Many of them, I happened to notice, were slipped inside protective sleeves made of transparent plastic. I could also see that they were full of equations, of some sort, as well as various symbolisms that I couldn't make any sense of at all.

I did, however, spot two equations that looked kind of familiar, and so I copied them down afterward so that I would be able to look up their meanings at a later time. As Burt was searching intently through the pages, he began telling me a story of how there were other alchemists whom he had been in contact with for many years now. These alchemists, he explained, shared a common interest in the type of experimentations he had been working on over all of these years. He apprised me of the fact that some of these people were prominent members in our society who cannot, for one reason or another, allow certain interests or personal ideals to be exposed, and so for this reason they remain vigil (doing what they can, when they can) while keeping a low profile.

Some of these men, he adds, have been guarding secrets longer than I've been alive, and are not inclined to share them, "no matter *who* you are or what pursuits you are after." To actually get one of them to free up some tid bit, evidently is cause for excitement.

Burt was adamant about keeping his alchemical pursuits as quiet as he could. Which was why it was so surprising to see him in such a frenzy over it, speaking to me as if he and I had been taking part together all along. Which I had only *recently* learned that I *had* been.

I then remembered how he had said to ask him about the cash "tomorrow," and so I did. However, when I *had* brought it back up, it became clear that he was not going to fill me in. He said something very vague about the fact that he had owed a friend from the area some money, and since we were coming here anyway he was just taking advantage of the opportunity to settle a debt. Burt had always told me everything that he believed I needed to know, the details in this particular situation unfortunately did not fall in that category.

He told me that now that he had *these* specific experiments, he would next have to take some time to properly examine them and attempt to decode them. Burt went on to say that if things were to go as planned, he will no longer lack any of the necessary elements to carry out this one particular experiment, one that he has waited so many years to attempt. He said that the potential to transmutate the body and soul from that of an imperfect state to an enlightened being who is one with all things, "could *theoretically* soon be within his grasp."

He also admitted to me that I was brought along for reasons that were all part of a plan. He said there was a sharp lesson to be learned from the experience, and I agreed that there was much to be taken from it. I was meant to experience what Larry does and why he does it, but most importantly who he does it for. Burt saw that I was in a phase of recovery where I needed to be reminded of life's frailty and the importance of each minute that passes. He also wanted me to understand how important it is that we give back to our communities, wherever it is most needed.

I had come to know Burt pretty well by this time, aside from what he didn't want known. That, and maybe a few more eccentricities that he still had hidden up his sleeve, but it was for this reason that I could tell when he wanted me to take a lesson from something. I had also gotten to this mindset where I was able to pinpoint just what it was that he wanted me to take notice *of.*

I stopped at a rest area and we swapped seats again. I told him that I didn't want to drive in my neighborhood with the police being well aware of my suspended license. Even when I did get my license back, they were still pulling me over, because it had just been so long that I had gone without one that everyone had just gotten used to it.

Soon we were pulling up to my house, and I was pushing for Burt to come in and play a quick game of ping pong, *hoping* to get the real scoop about these documents. Ping pong would normally do the trick, as he knew he could whip my ass. He declined though, and expressed his excitement about getting back and analyzing his file, which I already knew was going to be the answer.

So Burt left, off to solve the mysteries of the universe, and I ran in and set about trying to remember the equations that I had spotted while he was flipping through his 'secret' papers. The first one that I had remembered $S=k \log W$, I quickly found out, is a simplified mathematics expression of the universal law which explains how things have the tendency to move from order to disorder, increasing as time progresses. This involves the intensely technical science of thermodynamics, as well as theories first introduced by Ludvig Boltzmann, way back in the 1800's. The equation is referred to as Boltzmann's entropy equation, and is one of the most famous equations in physics.

This simple expression represents an entire universes continuity, and our existence as part of it. It also strikes familiarity in most addicts, as having experienced plenty of 'disorder' first hand, as well as it's tendency to get worse with time. Although, while that is not exactly what the equation is truly expressing, the words do still ring true.

The second equation that I had remembered was $t=t_0/(1-v^2/c^2)^{1/2}$. This one was of a different perspective, expressing the universal law that states, the faster something moves through space, the slower it moves through time. Now this law is just as fascinating and more. It affects all sorts of high-tech innovations, like GPS systems and satellites for instance, which would not be able to function without it.

This law expresses the fact that if you were to be able to take a set of twin babies, and raise one here on earth while simultaneously raising the twin brother/sister up in orbit, when compared next to each other after some time, the twin that was raised in space would be younger than the twin that was raised here on earth. Einstein was able to revolutionize the world by having the genius to see the universe in this fashion. This allowed him to observe these constants, and subsequently express them with mathematics in a way unthinkable to most.

$$\infty$$

What exactly it was that these equations had to do with whatever Burt was working on, had become a mystery to me. Although Burt and I did continue to meet up as always, he was noticeably changing little by little. He seemed to become far less outgoing and revealing absolutely nothing to me in regard to his research, or how it was that he happened to be rich for a day. Each effort I had made to inquire was met with sharp indifference. He would just shoot me down instantly. I got the hint, but I was left confused.

That is how things went for months. We'd meet up, discuss *my* life and the how's and why's of whatever had gone on since we had last parted ways, and that was it. He really seemed to be morphing as far as his general attitude was concerned. When only just recently he had been bubbly and talkative, he now remained more guarded and timid.

I did express my concern many times, to which he assured me "everything's cool," as he put it. That is until one day when I had asked if everything was OK, and instead of the usual brush off, he leaned in, spoke in a hushed tone and said that he was "getting near completion." I wasn't sure what he was talking about at first, because it had been so long with nothing said. I just assumed he had given up on his experiments.

Super Dope

One aspect of addiction which many individuals appear to think little of, is that nowadays words like "substance abuse" and "recovery" are now synonymous with big business. For example, my television is constantly bombarding me with ads for residential treatment programs, medicinal treatments, IOP's (intensive out-patient programming), and referral sites. With a good deal of the country experiencing opiate epidemics, all of this sparks the interest of the financially motivated. Any time there is a large group of people consumed by *any* topic, there is sure to be a million different angles thought of to profit from it.

The race to grab up profit dollars from the poor and unfortunate has gotten to the point that they have now begun outsourcing correctional responsibilities, which, in other words means that when an individual is sentenced to serve time in prison, the facility that they wind up in *could* perhaps be owned by a private agency. This then transforms the inmate, who is merely trying to repay a debt to society, into a commodity, like something one would buy and sell on the stock market. These privatized incarceration companies have studied the system quite thoroughly and have devised the absolute cheapest most effective methods technically possible, to ensure that these human warehouses continue to turn a profit. With numerous investors watching closely, those in charge will feel the pressure to cut spending down even further. So, this will result in cheaper, smaller meals, lower quality health care, and other budget cuts of the same nature. There are just too many spoons in the pot.

When researched, one finds that it's mostly our politicians who are the key shareholders in these corporations that continue to *win* the correctional contracts. The resulting effects are situations like we have going on now, where these same politicians are lobbying for tougher sentencing laws in an effort to send more customers their way. *All of this is public record for those who would like to learn more.*

We are certainly caught in a trend like never before. The rate at which our incarceration percentages are rising, reflect that the process of jailing us has become more efficient, while the process of rehabilitating us has all but failed. Our country has more people incarcerated than all of the other world powers combined. The United States also has approximately four times that of the NATO member with the second most incarcerated. With only 2% of the world's population and 25% of the world's incarcerated population, and they are on the hunt for more. That is why they continue to build more state of the art prisons, while allowing children to attend dilapidated schools and receive less than adequate education. With our country losing the race for advancement, one is forced to wonder how it is that we continue to allow this sort of trend to occur. I have heard it explained like this, the United States government always gets what it wants. They are getting what they are paying for, and if they wanted better students they would certainly pay for it.

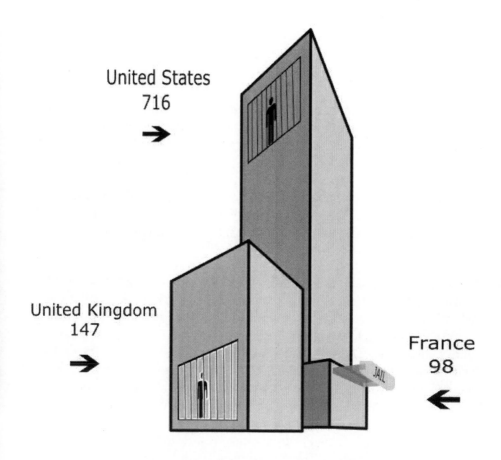

United States
716
→

United Kingdom
147
→

France
98
←

Incarceration Rates Among World Powers
(times 10,000 prisoners)

So then, what we must now try to understand is *why*? Why *wouldn't* they want better students? Well, that will always depend on who you are asking. I'm not attempting to steer anyone in any political directions here. I am merely saying that we need to keep our eyes wide open to what goes on. I aim to school those who have not seen the world in this light and perhaps reignite something buried deep inside them that still yearns for a better tomorrow. Once we see things as they truly are, we are able to form an idea of what it is that will help ourselves to tear free from these old and ineffective

175

thought patterns. We've got to *see* ourselves becoming whatever it is that we desire deep down, and as we come to practice *this* action more frequently, we find that we begin to change inside. While, one can not change the world overnight, we can change *ourselves* over time, and as a result, change the world in the end.

Every day there are people out there making very important decisions in regards to the opiate addict, who literally have no true knowledge of the situation at hand, and quite honestly don't want to. The problem is that they have no working knowledge due to the fact that all of the addicts *with* the pertinent information, are out there using, dying, incarcerated, in treatment, etc. Where you wont find the typical addict, is on Capitol Hill explaining whats *really* going on. The politicians realize this and are able to use it to their advantage, because *we're* not paying attention. This is the truth of the matter, and it is what goes on day after day.

Although, we've all done things when *they* weren't looking as well. The point I would like to make here is that this situation is not necessarily the fault of the politicians. When it comes to addressing just how it is that things have gotten to be this way, the blame lays squarely on our own shoulders. Politics are a sneaky, deceitful, and sometimes unjust world, but they are for the most part transparent, as we have full access to most everything that goes on now. The internet has revolutionized the way in which we can stay connected, allowing an individual to get up to the minute details on literally any subject of interest. It is our responsibility to seek this information out. Or don't. But we can not blame the government if *we* choose not to get involved, or we fail to make an effort to change things. Government is a necessary element to a functional society, I will be the first to admit this. Greed *is* a big part of human nature however, and so it becomes a situation where, 'if the cat's away the mice *will* play.'

I feel fortunate that I have been enlightened on matters such as these, and I can make an effort to help as many as I can to see that when it comes to opiate addiction, the deck is stacked. However, if those whom I have helped to guide do not do the same, or are just not affected emotionally by these problems, then how do we stop the problems? How do we reach those who do not want to be reached, or just aren't aware that they need to be? Of course this has been the million dollar question for as long as there have been men with their own opinions. I am not sure that there is an answer to the question, per se, but there are options to explore that can remedy the problem and hopefully bring about enough change that'll keep us in the fight.

Perhaps you have found all the assistance that you had required to turn your life around. If this is the case, then please, use what you have learned to help others who have not yet found what they need to achieve success. I am ready and willing to work at helping those who want it. I also look to assist those who may not realize that they need help, to see where it is that this path that they are on ultimately leads to. But *I* need help. All of this became partly the reasoning behind founding the ASBSF (Association for Small Business Seed Funding). I am going to need all the assistance I can get in order to successfully support this cause. As you will read, I have included a chapter which goes into detail regarding the ASBSF and what it's about, a little further on into the text. I believe in this cause unwaveringly, and I am focused on seeing it succeed. I encourage anyone who is able to join in and work together to ensure a brighter future for all of us.

It is of the utmost significance that we unite as recovered addicts and ex-cons, and create for ourselves a voice loud enough to be heard all the way up to the very top. We have got to speak up and tell the world exactly what it is that we need and want for our lives to be successful. It is important to understand that there are a great many people out there who do want to see you succeed, and not every politician is necessarily negative towards the opiate addict and his ability to rehabilitate. In fact, the situation is really quite the opposite. There are numerous politicians who are pushing to *lighten* the outdated punitive measures that have been in effect for decades.

We MUST educate any and all of those that we can reach who are on the wrong path or are in danger of *taking* the wrong path (in this instance wrong path = substance abuse). We must also ask that those whom we are sharing knowledge with, do the same when *they* are up to the task. Just think, if we truly could put a stop to this trend simply by coming together and declaring to no longer play part to it, this would most certainly be a change for the ages. We *can* become one as we collectively focus our attention on enhancing each and every one of our lives together, sharing information, opportunities, and assistance. We all want results. Like a decent job for instance, or a nice home to raise your children in. This is all within your grasp (no matter who you are), I promise. You've just got to want it and have the drive to make it happen.

Structure

I have included a few seemingly innocuous tales of my past, with an heir of humor sparsed throughout. However, I want to make clear that this is to help those readers who need it, reflect on the chaotic occurrences in their own lives and perhaps gain an ability to recognize the lunacy of it. These are not the goings on of a normal person, and if you *can* relate to them, you are in need of help I assure you.

In the early days of Burt and I getting together, we mostly just hung out and shot the breeze about random things. We told each other stories from our pasts and how we came to be who we are. As time went on however, these "sessions" morphed into something else altogether. We began to structure the time, choosing to limit our chit-chat so that we could focus on whatever issues *I* was facing at that time. I was struggling when I began to make my way toward a new life, and Burt seemed to just have this uncanny insight into the various issues I would be presented with all the time. I had done so much damage to my body, my soul, my mind, and my home/family life, that sifting through the wreckage and salvaging whatever I possibly could had become a full-time position.

I must clarify, that I did not *just* want to be sober. I wanted to swap out my entire existence thus far, for one of success, financial comfort and a quality family life. Burt was able to tune into these ideas of mine from the very beginning, and had developed a keen understanding of why I had them. I believe that he was probably able to do this with most people, though I had always felt as though he truly wanted to see *me* achieve success. It soon became clear that he saw my situation in just the right light that enabled him to zero in on the exact facets that weren't getting the proper attention, as well as the methods with which to address them.

I was not made aware of Burt's pursuits regarding things like spiritual rejuvenation or alchemy for quite some time. In my eyes, we were just two friends who were helping each other out (with myself needing a bit more help than he). Of course, when I had learned of his motivation it had taken me a little by surprise, but aside from explaining a lot of questions I had had, it didn't affect my opinion of him or my desire to continue on working with him in the slightest. My very existence had been altered for the better thanks to Burt's unique assistance. He had inspired me in a way that nobody else could. How could I argue with the results I ask you? I couldn't.

Meditation

This is a crazy mixed up world we've got going on here. In the last half hour I have seen an interview with Randy Quaid (the actor) and his wife, pleading to the media that there is a ring of pedophiles running Hollywood, and how celebrities are being "whacked" and extorted by the 'Illuminati' (or *some* secret society). It was immediately after I had watched that, when I had stumbled upon an article about one of Google's Deepmind projects, to create a network of computers with artificial intelligence capable of developing their own encryption ciphers and using them to communicate with each other. These are codes that are uncrackable by humans, enabling the network of A.I. machines to mask their own formulated communications without human eavesdroppers ever being able to make any sense of it.

Bearing in mind the complexity of our world these days, it becomes clear that it is going to take everything you've got to navigate your way around the intensity of it all and on down a path to success. You are going to benefit most if you can adapt to a mindset that allows you to re-experience the world with a fresh and *sober* attitude, and, in a sense, that same kind of innocence you once knew as a child. Make an effort to rekindle interests in inspiring curiosities.

Allow the energy to flow freely back and forth, from you to the universe and from the universe to you. It is through *this* principle that you will one day see things as you once did, back when the world was a complete mystery. Back to that point in your youth, when the simplest of things could amaze you and inspire you to reach continuously further. When you come to a point where you are able to envision yourself achieving new heights, you are then of a much more open frame of mind to begin zeroing in on whichever particular path you will soon call your own.

The objective here is for you to dig deep into your soul, locate that passion for life which once fueled your motivation to succeed, and find just what it is that you have been called to do with the rest of your time here. To *essentially* go back to when you were at the crossroads of life, and mentally take the opposite of what you once perceived to be the right path. From there you would then proceed to systematically addressing the various decisions you once thought were true and sure, as you take to mentally ascending through the stages of your life, playing out these 'decisions,' and allowing your inner self to be altered, as you come to understand which areas of your situation are in most need of attention. By allowing your spiritual self a chance to enjoy the energy needed to make a change for the better, the direction with which you will soon take your life reveals itself at such time that you are prepared to acknowledge it. These are objectives which will have to be worked out over time, as you begin to learn how to make effective use out of your time spent in therapy as well as during daily meditative thought.

Try to imagine your life in sobriety as that of a game of chess. In chess, you must analyze each move and its consequential effects, mentally playing out the results several moves ahead. Taking on this kind of perspective and maintaining it *can* enhance the individual's the ability to make productive decisions routinely. While many have sought to adapt this mindset to their lives, likening *sobriety* to the game has been spoke of very little.

As unique as you may feel your situation is, understand that what you are experiencing is an age old condition that has plagued our country ever since it was first formed. You are not doomed to this life. It is simply the result of a few select decisions you unknowingly made long ago. It goes far beyond the decision to experiment with a drug. When analyzed, many addicts' individual scenarios show that there was a decision to ignore a mental or physical ailment at some crucial point in their pasts, and the inherent need to provide relief of its effective symptoms. You might think of it like a computer virus. The computer does not contract a biological virus as a human would, but it is more of a virus in 'theory,' just as addiction is a disease, in theory.

∞

So you are on your computer one afternoon, trying to download some free music from one of those free mp3 sites, when you notice an ad box asking if you would like to hear more free music selections that are similar to your choices so far. Without much thought put into it, you click on it. Then, over time you begin to notice that your PC is running rather sluggish. Soon you are having issues downloading or opening programs, and ultimately it gets to the point that you can barely play a video, if at all. Now you must go through a series of steps to try and undo the damage that you aren't even clear on when or how it occurred. If you are not savy in such matters, you may even call in a professional. Often times it is necessary to wipe the entire hard drive clean and start all over from scratch, often losing much data in the process. And all of this, due to one deceivingly innocent mouse click, or, 'decision' to click the mouse.

When we consider the computer, we know that deep in that hard drive lies the truth. The truth of how, why, when, where, and who was responsible for the damage. The PC, however, often can not tell us these details, because the virus has either disguised itself, or simply because we don't all speak code and don't understand what to look for.

Your body, mind, and soul have a type of code as well, and we typically don't speak that code either. That is not to say that one can not learn. Your brain sends messages like Trump uses Twitter, constantly. These messages carry within them the instructions on how to remedy whatever ails the body. All *we* as addicts in recovery must do now is listen. Just listen to your mind, your body, and your spirit. As you sober up they will be sending SOS's endlessly, and there are attached files within these messages that, once we discover the correct 'program' to open and read them (meditation), we come to find that the solutions to all of these issues we each face have been there all along.

When we attain this kind of enlightenment and are in tune with ourselves, it is then that we develop the capacity to truly understand each and every decision and action that we as individuals engage in, as well as any long term effects that might result of it.

∞

185

You must learn that meditation is the most effective way to access this underlying world of good and bad decisions. Meditation is just as important as any other practice in this book. This is also another action that is affected heavily by your ego, and if your not careful you could endanger your chances at a sober life. You mustn't allow anything to stop you from mentally achieving a proper meditative state.

With sufficient effort and practice you *will* reach a point where you are able to allow your mind and body the freedom they need to achieve such levels of consciousness. As you will learn, this one act will become the tree that bears the fruit of knowledge, and more important, the knowledge that you seek. Perhaps not in the way in which you set about to find it, but more often than not from a rather unlikely source, revealed unexpectedly while in its pursuit.

This is the magic that will *always* happen. No matter who you are or what it is you seek, these methods will not fail those who see them through. If you find that this is not working out for *you*, then I assure you there is something in which you have not carried out thoroughly. My advice in this case is to go back, start again, and give it some time. Always permit time to do *its* part. This is the job of your life, so assign it the importance it deserves and allow for every possible detail. Open your mind and heart to the positivity, while keeping a vigil watch for the negative.

∞

The brain is capable of innumerable things, many of which are of no real control by us. One is trained to identify as a person with the thoughts that cross the mind. However, as Yogi mystic Sadhguru suggests, *we* as humans believe we *are* our thoughts. When we think or speak, we don't say "my brain tells me," instead, we say "I think so." Sadhguru reminds us that we do not have control over the brains actions in the same way that we can control other parts of the body, like the fingers for example. The brain is an internal organ, just as the liver or kidneys. Could *you* cause your liver to respond in any way, purely by thought? Of course not. You've got to consume something, let the stomach and digestive tract do its part, and then at some point beyond that the liver is triggered into action unbeknownst to us. We do not "control" it, it simply reacts to the substances ingested. This is a compulsive process, just as your brain has been acting on *its* own accord.

Our individual thoughts are emanations of the "stuff" (as Sadhguru calls it) that we as people consist of deep within. They are a reflection of all we have put into them, which he states, can often reflect the fact that many of us "have allowed our brains to become the rubbish bins of our lives." In order to attain an entirely conscious thought process, we must learn how to stop permitting ourselves to fill up on such unnecessary baggage.

However, as we have learned, we do not have the control over our thoughts that we may have once believed we did. Therefore we must now develop the aptitude to take control over what we allow *into* our individual brains. False and negative information, a poor diet, lack of exercise, and substance abuse, are all key issues to address if one expects to evolve from this state.

Burt had turned me onto Sadhguru for a specific reason back some time ago. I was having issues when I would attempt any form of meditation, where, I just could not seem to clear my mind. By suggesting that I look to Sadhguru about this, I had learned that I was going about the whole process all wrong, and that meditation is not done simply by clearing the mind (as this is just about impossible anyhow). One cannot stop the brain from operating. We've got to limit what we allow our individual minds to absorb, thereby eliminating the excess (non-productive) thought that is experienced when attempting to meditate. Once this is mastered, one finds that meditation comes far easier and with much longer lasting effects.

Sweatin' with an Oldie

Exercise is a bitch. If your not naturally inclined to tone your physique, it can be a huge pain in the ass to get going with it. But it's necessary. Even if you have limitations with your mobility, you **must** find some form of conditioning. Your body truly is your 'temple' as they say. It is *your* vessel that will carry your spirit until the day you die. It's gotten you this far, why not reward it with some attention.

First off, go to the pharmacy and look at the selection of digestive 'cleanses' that they offer. Read each of the labels, and find one that will work for your individual self. They differ in a number of ways, and so it is important that you first develop an understanding of how each one works. A cleanse like this will expel any residual toxins left in your body and leave you feeling much healthier, able to start your workout routine with a fresh detoxed system.

If you are anything like me, you've walked a million miles already during the process of hustling money and copping drugs. Well things are different now, and so although you *will* still need to walk some more, your mind will now be free to experience the world around you. Free to take in the scenery and co-exist with society, while allowing yourself to achieve peace and tranquility in the process. Try using this time as I do, to work out various issues of daily life that perhaps require some level of deep thought. As a matter of fact, I have found that I do most of my best writing while on foot.

You must develop a routine and stick to it. One trick that I had learned was to eat a small amount of something high in sugar just prior to doing anything active. It gives me just the right amount of pep (without feeling jittery), and allows me to complete the task at hand. Of course, they also have a zillion different energy bars, drinks, and supplements that are available as well.

Start with short walks around your area and gradually increase you out and distance traveled. This is where the mp3 player comes in, as th enhance your day immensely as well as make your exercise routines

Find whichever musical genre you enjoy, and then download a fair amount of songs or albums, or at least as much as your device can hold (without having memory issues). You are going to want a comfortable, quality set of headphones, and this is actually very important. You can get ear buds at the gas station nowadays for as little as five bucks, although these are cheap crap will not last and are not going to deliver the entire sound structure that you would get with a quality set. If and when you can, go the few extra bucks and get a quality device.

Soon you will have developed a routine of taking periodic walks throughout the day, no matter the weather. You will next have to begin seeking out a way to attain full body conditioning. I'm not going to suggest a specific routine or method, as this is going to vary to some degree depending on your individual situation. What I will suggest, is that you do find something and embrace it. If you have a YMCA near you, and you can afford it, get yourself a membership. Perhaps you have the funding to join a regular gym, and maybe even hire a fitness trainer. If this is the case, I would suggest that you compare the packages that the different gyms out there offer before you make a commitment.

I have found that when I need to work out, it's easiest if I first stretch a little bit, and then begin by doing laps around the gym or wherever I am. I'll go a couple of laps, do a set of reps of whatever I'm using at the time, take a big sip of water, and do a couple more laps. The walking helps keep the blood flowing, while the water helps to oxygenate the blood. Bit by bit, if you keep at it, the results will begin to appear rather quickly.

Many of us smoke cigarettes and drink coffee, perhaps more heavily
we embrace certain recovery programs, detoxes, and residential
s. You are going to have to eliminate these habits as you push
not easy, and will probably be the hardest thing you will ever

are doing here is we are attempting to quell the sub
busy. We have gotten accustomed to constantly
ustling, copping, driving/walking/busing/training,
yway you get the point. When we sober up,
s,' and more introspective thought and

190

focus. There is a huge gap left, creating utter boredom for the sub conscience. And so we smoke and we drink coffee, because these things are accepted and have become the norm at meetings, etc. It's as if we've become entirely dependent upon having something to do, that we must now stay constantly fixated on some other insignificant thing while letting the world pass us by unnoticed. Is this who we truly are? Or is there some other reason we remain in this 'numb' state of mind?

Burt had explained it like so, he said that many will use fixations like this as a means to avoid introspective thought, so as not to face certain personal 'demons.' It is your responsibility to determine which category you fall under and address it accordingly. If you are avoiding inner issues there is simply no chance at all of achieving any real personal growth. In other words, if you do not take care of whatever it is you are avoiding, you will continually carry on in this fashion. This can no longer work for us. These are unhealthy habits, especially when done to excess. If we are to become something better, these are some of the key issues which we are going to have to address.

My suggestion is a reflection on Burt's opinion of the matter, which is to say that, if we still find that we must be fixated on *something,* then try swapping out the fixations once again. Only now you would select something far less dangerous, like chewing gum or sucking on lozenges. Even if you must begin with the nicotine gum and work your way to regular gum from there. The idea, clearly, is to choose something that is not going to be as harmful to your body. What *should* happen is, after a while the new fixation will begin to wane. Although you may have to chew gum forever, the health benefits of quitting cigarettes will be worth it. When life becomes enjoyable we realize that maybe we'd like to stick around for a while. In order to make this happen, changes must take place.

The objective to all of this body conditioning is not to create a 'He-Man' of yourself, but instead to mold yourself into a toned, well oiled machine. That is *what* your body is, a machine, and it requires some basic maintenance and TLC. As you engage in fitness activities more often, you will find that your mood will be far more stable due to the release of endorphins. As your body works to repair itself, natural aminos will be pumping all throughout, and helping to alleviate pains.

If you cannot yet get yourself to an actual gym, you might try finding a partner to workout with, or set something up that enables you to watch workout videos on the internet. You can play them at your leisure, follow what *they* do, and before you know it, your done for another day. It will no doubt leave you feeling healthier, and perhaps even more outgoing. The benefits are going to be endless.

Section Three Wrap Up

This section is where the real bulk of the key issues lie. It is in this section that the individual should be:

- Gaining a better knowledge regarding medicinal treatments, as well as looking to begin whichever one suits your individual needs
- Coming to the realization that some type of therapy is going to be necessary
- Aware of the importance in making good use of the therapy sessions
- Aware of the danger involved in making sobriety announcements too soon
- Refraining from putting too much emphasis on sober dates
- Selecting and focusing on personal goals
- Selecting a reassessment date
- Aware of the importance in treating a relapse immediately and continuing on (no starting over)
- Starting to apply moderation toward all aspects of life
- Thinking about what hobbies might interest you
- Learning how to divide up the day into the most efficient and productive way for your own individual needs
- Discovering how to achieve a relaxed meditative state and regularly practicing
- Looking for an effective workout routine to fit your physical state

Section Four

The Meeting

Things were heating up right about this time as far as working at the plant. This was a result of the fact that I had gained some real recognition from a couple of the top dogs in the executive offices. They had asked that I come up and take care of some random tasks that they wanted done, and I had gotten right on it. It was basic stuff, like hanging a few "white boards," which are just big erasable boards for lectures, as well as building a small shelf for some projection equipment.

I had assumed that these executives weren't altogether handy, as they were "blown away" with the work that I had done and made it a point to inform my supervisors of their gratitude. Now, if you have ever seen the film "Office Space," there is a scene in which the "two Bob's" (the guys doing the layoffs) were explaining to the head boss "Lumberg" how *they* felt that Peter (the main character) was just "management material all the way." Lumberg, who was (essentially) Peter's nemesis, was not feeling it and was utterly refusing to accept the idea of it. Just then the Bobs pull out Lumberg's employee file and begin making inquiries into his own job and *it's* value to the company. Anyway, you can be certain that this is probably a pretty fair assimilation as to how Steve and Rob reacted to *my* being praised, but for the part where their files get pulled of course.

I was just happy to get noticed and I couldn't let myself become bothered with what these guys thought. However, all of this *had* sparked further tension between myself and the two of them, and they soon began resorting to devious tactics. For instance, I would take all of my breaks to smoke way out away from the main building. For a while, nobody even knew that I had been going out there. That is until one afternoon when Rob had spotted me. The very next morning, he began joking around with me and giving me a false sense of comfort, thereby gaining my trust somewhat in the process. I'll admit it was my own fault, I had marched myself straight into a trap.

So anyhow, Rob goes out of his way one morning and walks me over to a special gate, which he failed to mention was just outside of the head executives office window, and had shown me an area where he explained would be ideal for me to go and take my cigarette breaks. I agreed, it did look to be the perfect location. Still, I'm wondering why he suddenly cares where I smoke, or whether or not I enjoy it. Though that is what I did. Basically from that point onward that is where I went to take *all* of my smoke breaks. Well, as I had previously mentioned this was directly below the head chiefs office, as well as being an area that I was forced to use my key card to access. This meant that each time I would smoke a cigarette, it was documented electronically and right in front of the top dog's face. Any times that I might have grabbed an extra break, say, or taken a couple of extra minutes to come back from break, would all be well known to everyone . Not to mention the fact that often these days smokers are considered like pariahs to many people, and it might have created a negative light in the eyes of the corporate staff.

Albeit rather minor, these *were* still manipulations of my life with the intention of causing a negative effect. This type of behavior from a "supervisor" is unacceptable, and happens to give you an indication of the level of maturity within the individual. With these little manipulations occurring all the time now, it really had become increasingly difficult to feel at ease while on the job.

It's fair to say that things had become tense and it was beginning to really affect my days there. Where it was once a joy to wake up knowing that I had a good job that I loved, I now lost sleep many nights, my home life was suffering, and I had zero appetite whatsoever. These issues were taking a toll on my body, and Burt, who was well informed of everything going on, wanted to help in some way. I explained that there really wasn't anything *to* do about it. Nonetheless, he felt he should do the only thing he could think of, which was to come and meet me on my breaks, if for nothing more than support. He would come by here and there and just hang out with me for the short time that I would have, and then go about his way.

One particular morning he stopped by to visit real quick when someone in the executive office had spotted him out there with me, and then went as far as to make an inquiry regarding this to my supervisor, Steve. According *to* Steve this person hadn't said much, only that I was to report to Mr. Beechums office first thing upon his return from vacation, which I was told was to be six weeks from then. Frank Beechum was the CEO of the entire corporation at that time and so this was kind of a big deal in the eyes of my co-workers. I'll admit, I *was* having mixed feelings about having to go to this meeting and what would be said.

Supplemental Advice

One subject that I had learned about through Burt's instruction, was that there are a number of herbal and nutritional supplements out there that are extremely beneficial for an individual working his way toward a healthy happy lifestyle. I was shown various supplements and the specific effects each one can have on an individuals life, and the improvements in quality of life that I have witnessed are substantial.

However, the only way to ensure that one is getting quality products (these are not regulated by the FDA) is to purchase high quality rated brands. After researching all of the possibilities and creating a personal regimen, one finds that the expenses involved can skyrocket in no time at all. When the individual comes to acknowledge and feel the improvements that these can make in their life, they are faced with a situation where they are sacrificing funds from bills or what have you, as a way to keep up with the cost of maintaining their program. This should not be the case however, and I have since been seeking a way to get around it.

I happen to know first hand just how important these supplements can be to someone's quality of life. I have also experienced the woes of not being able to afford them month in and month out. So, I am using my website www.thestonedphilosopher.net as a forum for delivering you the most up to date information on new findings, product comparability, and product pricing. I will be seeking out the best products that offer both quality *and* affordability, and I will then use any support I've garnered through this book and this site to advocate for a *special* lower pricing bracket that would be for available for people like us, as individuals who are attempting to rebuild our lives and are faced with very limited resources. Because these types of things are over the counter, there is almost zero funding or assistance of any sort available to those who cannot afford them. I do know that some insurance companies will cover certain supplements if your doctor prescribes them, but this is a very short list.

This is just another example of how we as addicts in recovery could benefit by coming together as a unit. By upping our numbers *as* a unit, we can overcome far more obstacles than an individual ever could accomplish alone. A company that deals in these types of products is going to be far more likely to engage in some kind exclusivity and discount pricing deal, if I can prove that I have X number of potential customers who will purchase from their company alone, or at the very least predominantly. The way we achieve this, is for you to use the website to show your support and spread the word as well as the link.

One footnote here, is that I encourage any and all of you who have information and experience with herbal and nutritional supplements and would like to share your findings, to please log on to the site and share your knowledge with others. This is how we learn and rise above these struggles that we all face, by sharing information and experience so that the next man (or woman) has a leg up.

To the Folks / A Point of Vantage

If you are reading this book as a concerned parent, thank you. There should be many more like you, but unfortunately the ugly truth of the matter is that there really just aren't. I am glad to help anyone who is making an effort to keep their loved ones far away from the reaches of this deadly disease. The way we do this, is to give them every bit of information that we can on the subject and help them to understand the consequences of what can sometimes appear to be utterly mundane decisions.

Typically, or the way it had used to be (before the internet), exposure to the more harmful elements in life came at a slower pace. While I can not speak well enough informed regarding the complexities of the situation now and just *how* much faster that exposure rate can be, it is clear that it has increased. Hopefully, with security measures and parental blocks, the situation is not so severe that we have lost the ability to make an impact on it. I would strongly urge all of you parents out there to tighten up security measures regarding the internet, and do your part to help keep the wolves away from the sheep.

The time honored remedy to this, is to keep an open line of communication with your children. I can attest that this is by far your first (and best) line of defense. When you are in tune with their lives, it becomes much easier to take notice when something appears to be off. And with an open relationship, they will be more likely to confide in you when questioned on the matter. Be sure to take an interest in any shred of enthusiasm that they show toward any topic, no matter how ridiculous you may think it is. It is from these "shreds" (sometimes) that the child finds his or her direction in life.

Understand that todays children are up against a fight to keep clear of drugs like no other time or place before us. The availability and widespread frequent use is unimaginable. I believe that by now, it's near impossible for a child to live to the age of fifteen and not have crossed paths with opiates in one way or another. To me, this is a tragic affair that requires immediate attention. Each hour that we waste, another 5.25 lives are lost and I am left but to wonder why? How?

How is it that our country can land a rover on Mars, but apparently can not make even a slight dent in the several pounds (sometimes tons) of heroin that manage to cross the borders each day? Enough, so that just about every town and every city throughout every state of our entire country, consistently has an unending supply that is amply feeding the daily demand. A demand that continues to increase in number as time progresses.

I am not attempting to spew conspiracy theories here, but I can't seem to make any sense of it at all? I'm just asking as a concerned citizen, where are the results?

If you happen to be a dealer or were at one time, I'm not trying to condemn you or put you down, but understand that I have had many people who were close to me die, and while that was a choice that *they* had made, the dealers are not helping the situation any. Please get a degree or certificate of some sort, and find another line of work. I do understand that many are part of certain minority groups and face struggles that are unique to their ethnicity. I also acknowledge the plight of growing up a minority in the hood. I've been on the streets and have put my time in at the penitentiary. I've also done my research and acknowledge the existence of the underlying struggles that many turn a blind eye to, such as redlining, liquor lining, sundown towns (not so much these days), voter suppression, and mass incarceration to name a few.

Many do not understand the situations that the folks from these impoverished areas continually face. They step out their door and every white kid that passes by is asking where the drugs are, flashing wads of cash in a place where cash is king. In a damaged economy, lacking in employment opportunities, the money talks.

The point I would like to make, however, is that there are still many options available. Nowadays there are increasingly more options available to those from low income areas, and this I *know* to be a fact, as an addict and ex-con I had once fit the category. You've got to seek them out of course, but there is help available in most areas. It depends on your motivation. If you truly are a businessman at heart and possess some unique sales skills, I assure you that you are wasting your talents in the drug game. You could be making just as much and more without subjecting yourself to all of the risk involved in selling drugs, in an actual legitimate field. However, you must first sell your *best* asset, yourself. Apply your sales strategy when attempting to gain employment, and sell the idea of yourself becoming a valuable asset to the company for which you are applying.

∞

Now we've all seen the reality series' that showcase specific types of narcotics investigations, like where they're busting the people with drugs as their coming off of the planes for instance. Let's break down exactly what it is they are showing us here. For starters, it is always cocaine or marijuana. I've rarely, if *ever*, seen them arrest someone with heroin or *any* opiates of any real value. Secondly, it is always the petty 'mules' that they are arresting, who you know will *die* if they were to flip sides and begin working with the detectives. Still yet, I watch as they assure them safety and protection, often using overly comforting methods right up until they've gotten what they need. These upper level drug dealers have an unending supply of resources to seek these people out. After the DA gets what *they* want, these poor folks (who were probably doing this to feed their family and are scared to death of prison) are in a tense situation for sure. I just wouldn't want to *have* to rely on the government to keep me hidden for the rest of my life, but of course who would?

What I would like to know is where are the *large* quantity *heroin* busts? The big busts. The ones where the guys who are stuffing the mules (those who transport drugs) go down for a change? Please, somebody tell me where? I had once gotten caught up mistakenly in a sting operation, without having any drugs or ties to any illegal activity, and still, I had *my* picture on the news along with two hundred and something others. The local news flaunted our pictures, touting large figures of cash and material that the sting had removed from the streets, when in reality what they had was three hundred addicts, a collective amount of evidence that *sounded* good enough, and not one actual dealer. The majority of these cases were thrown out, and nobody rolled over on their suppliers. But the people who are watching this on the news are not *aware* of any of these things, and upon hearing the stats of it would probably assume that it meant *progress*. What it *was*, was a precisely calculated execution of a plan of action decided by a select few who remain far from the field of battle. It was an expected result to a thoroughly thought out plan.

The detectives were pulling up to the soup kitchens in disguise, asking if anyone wanted to make a few extra bucks by finding them a couple of bags (of heroin). This was of course a rough area, and a great many people sell drugs around there (with heroin being the most *commonly* sold drug). It is second nature to a lot of the people from this particular neighborhood, right from the (sometimes pre-) teens on up. I know that I personally have bought heroin in this neighborhood, from a child that was young enough to be my son (and this was when I was fifteen years younger). Anyway, with this being the case, no matter who it is, they're bound to know *someone* that does sell dope, and they could most assuredly use the money as well. A couple of bags sounded innocent enough, and there it is. One minute they're helping some stranger to get off "E," and the next they're in jail on a bail they'll never post, and beginning another journey into the world of incarceration on a charge of 'distribution.' It's a joke, only we're not on the right end of it.

It is still a good thing, in some respect, to try and create in those who are coming to your city to cop drugs, a fear that may help keep them away. This could, I suppose, over time result with the dealers eventually choosing another line of business, or, at the very least, another location. But that is a very long shot. There will be customers no matter how many you bust, because they often make bail anyway and are back on the block within hours.

The dealers however, well, they tend to face much more serious charges when they are taken in, as well as much larger bond amounts. Now, if this truly were a numbers game and the funding to combat these problems was a legitimately important issue, then the logical plan of action would dictate that the authorities focus the bulk of their attention on the dealers, as opposed to the addicts. This, due to fact that, first of all, there are nowhere near as many dealers as there are addicts. Not to mention the impact that removing the dealers could have on the neighborhoods that they are destroying. If this were an actual a war of combat, you can be certain that this is where the victorious general would have struck the hardest. It is simple common sense, yet the complete opposite of what has been done for years on end now. I'm not going to pretend to know why *exactly* it is that they do what they do, but I do understand what I've been witness to, as well as the results of all of these "methods," and I would be putting it mildly by saying, *I'm not impressed.*

Many will be quick to point out that the detectives and district attorneys *use* these addicts, to gain information that ultimately leads to the apprehension of higher level dealers. However, I personally do not agree with turning someone who has had a run of bad luck, often unwittingly, into a bulls eye for gang members, inmates, and ex-cons of all sort, by asking them to provide information or testimony. Those who are addicts should be asking themselves if they feel comfortable knowing that it is possible that they have been playing right into the hands of some bloated corporate mega mind, who has designs on imprisoning as many as possible, in order to turn their retail lock-up institutions into USDA prime cash cattle.

∞

This did not come to be by accident. This is the norm, day in and day out. In order for you to make *some* sense of it, you must first understand that if they were to bust all of the dealers, there would be no one to move the product. Without any more dealers to keep the product moving, there are no longer any assets to seize, no fines or court costs to collect from the addicts, and no bodies to fill the beds at these state of the art prisons that they continue to build. Following the domino effect we see that this also means a loss of jobs for C.O.'s, as well as a loss of pay for the sheriff. Before too long employment opportunities in the correctional *and* probation areas would just about dry up altogether. As we follow the money trail, we learn that there would no longer be any need for methadone or bupenorphine treatments, detox units (alcohol only), or any other drug treatment centers for profit or *otherwise.*

Without addicts there to jam up the legal system nice and tight with plenty of fresh cases, public defenders would no longer be overworked and over burdened, hence allowing them time to sufficiently represent their clients and actually win a case for a change. I have rarely in my life had the luxury of a paid attorney representing me. As a result, this afforded me the pleasure of working countless times with the bar advocates, of which not one has ever attempted to mount any sort of defense tactic in my favor.

What the bar advocates *will* do, is introduce themselves to you while your there at the court house. They will often times have a brief chat with you and attempt to put your mind at ease as best they can with talk of filing motions and getting this or that dropped, but this will almost never happen. What is the more likely scenario to occur, assuming your in lock-up, is: first, they assure you that they will be 'up to the jail to see you soon,' which almost never happens either. They will then usually give you a card with a phone number on it, that you are supposed to be able to call from the jail and attempt to prepare your defense, but this line requires that they put money on the account and they almost, no, they *never* do that.

Upon your first pretrial hearing, they will come down to the bullpen and have a brief talk with you. This occurs in front of everyone else (other inmates), which I feel is a violation of your rights in itself. This makes it so that you are unable to hear, due to the noisy people in the same and other cells. The attorney quickly reads the charges off and then the police report, usually for the first time right then. They next inform you about the record that you already knew you had. And then, based on this record, they will next attempt to entice you with the shortest possible sentence that they can wrangle from the D.A. (district attorney), using an agreement by you to dispose of the case that day as leverage.

This works out well for the court, as it gets the defendant behind bars (on paper anyway) for the cheapest amount possible, without, mind you, the ever important burden of proof. Often times, if the defendant is serving a separate sentence, they offer to run the charges concurrent, adding no extra time onto the existing sentence. I have had them work around my own 'out date' multiple times, in an effort not to disrupt my day to go home. This of course succeeds in enticing me to go ahead and proceed with it. Why not? If it doesn't affect my time and it's all done with, it would seem like a good option. Not to mention the effect the bullpen can have on an individual's decision to just get it over with. This is referred to as 'bullpen therapy,' and is a very real, very calculated experience.

Here I sit, twenty years forward with a mountain of convictions and the blatant inability to secure employment that is sufficient to support a household. I recently had talked with an attorney whom, though he was not representing me, went ahead as a favor and took a look at my record along with the transcripts from some of my cases. He then informed me that had I been able to afford representation back when I was facing these various charges, I would never of had to plea to even half of them. However, as I had already said, not one public defender has ever suggested that I not take the deal and instead fight the charges.

∞

From the vantage point of someone who has had plenty of time to study it (criminal justice system), it would appear as though things are certainly set up the way they are for a reason. Essentially, to get exactly what it's getting. If it wasn't effective and useful to somebody, you can bet they would soon change it. I would like for you to ask yourself whether or not you honestly believe that *each* court is entirely unable to hire a couple of extra bar advocates? I am certain that I'm not the first one to realize that this is all it would take to give the downtrodden an even remotely fair shot at achieving actual justice. To this one might ask then, why, if I have already admitted to committing crimes on the daily, should I have been concerned with *fighting* cases. Assuming then that I should have just admitted guilt whenever I felt I *was* guilty. And that is what I thought as well, which is the reason why I had gone along with this process for so long.

However, just because I know I've done something wrong, does not take away from the fact that the prosecutor is still faced with the burden of proof. It had taken me a long time to understand the principle of this. These days it seems that even the younger ones are more hip to this truth right from the very start. This being a result of the courts today consistently seeing more serious crimes committed by younger and younger defendants. You meet a lot of guys in their late teens and early twenty's in the system, both county *and* state (I've never been to federal, though I've heard it's the same everywhere). It's no thing for a teen to have a gun conviction now, and/or a bullet wound for that matter. I know that *I* could name off twenty guys that I know right now that have gun wounds from their younger days, and probably twice as many that have carried guns (illegally).

This is the sad truth of it, but it doesn't have to be so for *our* young ones. Thanks to greed and selfishness, the youth of tomorrow will be coming up behind us facing the struggles of *our* creation. We have got to each make an effort to reach out and help those around us who are in need, and try and undo some of the damage that has already been done. However, this is going to require the cooperation of each and every one of us if we are expecting to see results on a *national* scale.

As the equation $S = k \log W$ stated, it's with time that the likelihood of any situation progresses from order to disorder. Which means, the longer we procrastinate the inevitable grand effort that we will one day be forced to make, the more probable it is *mathematically* that our problems will exist two-fold at the very least.

Whether your an addict (in recovery) who wants to give back to your community, a family member of an addict and would like to help out, or perhaps just a concerned citizen, there is certainly *something* that you could do to improve the world around you. Get involved with any cause that supports a better tomorrow for *all* of us.

Kung Fu and Pot

There is this cable channel called "El Rey," and I'm not even sure why they named it such, but anyhow every Thursday night this particular channel plays kung fu movies from the evening on through til the early morning. This was one subject which both Burt *and* I had a fair knowledge of. Although Burt's interest in kung fu films was from a different perspective than mine, we enjoyed hanging out together and watching them. Burt watched these films for the ancient alchemical references, that, until I began watching with him, had never really noticed. *I* simply watched because I like the fight choreography, as well as the visual scenery from old China.

So it was another week gone by, and Burt and I had met up as usual and talked for a while. We discussed the troubles I was having at work and the fact that I would now be forced to take whatever repercussions were coming my way as a result of having him hang out with me on my break. Though I did notice that he seemed oddly quiet about this particular topic. Anyway, he did appear to be in better spirits this time, so *that* was positive. He had asked if I wanted to watch that nights kung fu with him (it being a Thursday), and I was getting the impression that maybe he was finally coming out of whatever had been going on. I quickly agreed while he was in a good mood and told him to come on over whenever he was ready, I would be home (we always watched at *my* house).

It was about 7 pm when he had gotten to my place, which was just enough time before the first flick was starting for Burt to engage in his "preparations." For whatever reason, he's got this tradition where he likes to smoke a little pot before he watches. He really wasn't a big pothead at all and in fact he rarely *ever* smoked it. Except, however, when he watched kung fu. Aside from that I had only known him to smoke once in a great while, when he would be trying to take advantage of one of it's medicinal properties, of which he had often claimed he was once witness to actual verified results. I guess at one time he had been friends with a scientist of some sort who was an employee at Purdue Pharma (or one of those companies) down in Connecticut, and they had been involved together in research pertaining to marijuana's medicinal value. There were other interesting research topics that

214

this same individual had taken part in, but I could hardly follow when Burt would get ranting on about them.

According to Burt, marijuana is a treasure trove of possibilities. However, it was going to take some time for the scientists to isolate the numerous endocrines that he had informed me were locked within it's chemical structure. He explained how the laws surrounding marijuana over the years had made it near impossible for this to have occurred any sooner, but assured me that now that certain states are beginning to loosen the restraints regarding the laws surrounding marijuana, scientists are now being afforded the necessary parameters to complete these types of projects. He went on to say that they will likely one day cure cancer with pot.

When he was rolling his joint on the kitchen counter, he asked where the best place was to go "puff" (in an effort to avoid exposing me to the smoke). I told him there was no need and that I preferred if he just smoked in front of the tube where he was comfortable. It just didn't bother me. I insisted on this and he conceded with little effort.

I wasn't going to force the question, but he *had* recently informed me that he was nearing some kind of result with his research. He then said he was going to have me over soon, but it never happened. So I was purposely trying to steer the conversation towards that direction and having very little luck.

"Hey, what's been goin' on with the experiments?" I asked.

"It's hard to say exactly, I've been spending a lot of time working out all of the information I had gotten through *Rosenberg,* and it's just been a ton of material to get through" he replied.

Although this response *appeared* to be innocent, it was definitely premeditated. He apparently had jumped the gun back when he had told me that he was "nearing completion," which can happen to all of us at one time or another. Something begins to look promising, you get excited and want to share the news, and then you find that the situation is a little more involved than you had initially perceived it to be. It sounded as though he didn't want to get into it, and so I backed off.

So the first film to air was "Enter the 36th Chamber," and as we watched, Burt explained the various references to me while periodically taking a pull off his joint. As I was returning to the living room from answering a phone call, I had decided to take a toke off his joint, and so I asked him to pass it. Now this was a little odd, because his typical response would have been to try and talk me out of it. Though instead he just passed it.

By now it was a roach, and so we had to do the (E.T. phone home) finger pass, and, as we did there was an arc of electricity that shot from my finger to his, or vice versa. I do not have carpeting and I had never seen that happen before. To see that arc, it was oddly bright and blue, it struck me (literally) as being a bit bizarre.

We didn't think too much of this and continued on watching until the late hours, laughing and having a good time just chilling out. I had gotten the munchies, and went and bought a bunch of junk food at the corner store. Burt just laughed when I walked in and he saw all the crap that I had bought, and before long he began muttering random comments pertaining to the fact that he was tired and wanted to get on his way home.

He was still living in Jerry's refinished basement at this time. Though I had only been in the house the one time and had talked to Jerry only a couple of times, he seemed like a nice enough guy. For what he was doing for Burt, as far as renting him that unbelievable apartment for very little, I would say *that* made him a good guy for sure. Though I *would* catch Burt bitching to himself about Jerry every now and again, he never let on what it was about.

That night I had the most unusual dreams. Vivid, lucid dreams where I was in (what appeared to be) the 1700's. I was floating through this dark misty flame lit scenery of cobblestone roads, little huts with straw roofs, and faceless people who were draped with the kind of tattered rags you might to see in 18th century London.

I recall a strong scent, but could not place it at the time. I thought it was odd though, as I had never had a sense of smell in a dream before. There were wizard looking figures gathered around little campfires, who were formed into groups that appeared from above as creating a perfect shape. I then saw what I would describe as, elves, scurrying up trees with the same agility you would expect from a squirrel.

I began to notice the fact that my body was tiny, and I was encased inside something similar to a glass ball, when, for some reason, I noticed my reflection on the inside of the glass and I smiled. This caused me to *not* notice the head of a hammer come crashing into the ball, releasing me and causing me to drop, which is when I had awaken. As I was trying to fall back asleep, I couldn't get the image of the shape that the wizards appeared to be forming, out of my head. Somehow, I knew I had seen this figure before. I got up, grabbed a pencil and sketched it out. I soon fell back asleep and had all but forgotten about it.

The following morning, I tried to call Burt, as we usually checked in with each other at some point throughout the day. However, this particular morning I had gotten his voice mail on the first half of a ring. Burt's phone was never off and he had made it a point to stress that fact to me many times. He wanted me to feel free to call whenever I needed, as I believe he took pride in being a source of support for me and anyone else who needed him. I called a few more times with no luck and started to wonder if everything was OK. Something just felt off.

The (knee) Jerk

Out of all of the advice and information that I had acquired from my time working with Burt, one technique stands out as the single most effective tool yet. By adhering to this simple idea, I had developed the fortitude to beat this disease in a way that is unparallelled to any previous efforts. My thoughts about it initially were not entirely positive, as it had defied the logic of all that I had learned prior to that point. However, once I saw it through, I found that it very well may have been my saving grace.

What I am referring to, is the two-part lesson regarding a relapse trick of which I had spoke about in the first section. I explained that I would get to the second part further into the text, and so here it is: The first part of this idea is for the addict to subscribe to the notion that, when faced with depression over the absence of these substances, remember that you do not necessarily have to stop your opiate use *forever*. This is a depressing thought for any individual who has spent countless hours of their life obsessing over them.

Burt had shown me through this process how, when first getting clean and fighting all of the after effects that come with this, we as addicts are not in a stable frame of mind to combat the disease's efforts to pull us back in. So why not (in a sense) fool the brain temporarily, as a way to quell the initial depression experienced. This would therefore help to avoid any relapsing due *to* the depression. What will happen is, when and if you do reach a point where you have made your way through a good portion of these important goals *of* which you will have previously outlined, and are ready to reassess (which I spoke about in the first part of this process), you will find that if you consider all of the angles of going ahead with it and intoxicating yourself with your D.O.C. (drug of choice), there is an overwhelming list of reasons that you can come up with to *not* go through with it. This is only apparent if you make the decision to stop, take a step back, and take stock of the situation.

It is probable that you *will* still want to get high. Although, filled with positivity and visions of achievable goals which had been nonexistent until recently, your conscience should have a hard time with the idea of jeopardizing what you have already accomplished thus far. Assuming you have been on track and focused for an ample length of time, you **will** then be inundated with feelings of success, achievement, and self-respect. You should be more able to now foresee the cause and effect of these choices. Essentially, you will have a better understanding regarding the 'endgame' of the decision as a whole.

When I had reached the point in my own recovery where I had planned to reassess this situation, I thought to myself, although I do not want to turn my back on my sobriety *now*, perhaps a little further down the road I might feel differently. So I then elected to choose another reassessment date. This day would come and go as well, and still I remained sober. By this time I had had even *more* to lose, and if you yourself truly take a look at the situation from a rational point of view, you really ought to come to the same realization.

There is something far more meaningful about making our *own* decision to remain drug free. When things wind up getting out of hand and we are forced into sobriety (incarceration), we sometimes feel like we've been cheated and hence this drive to get back to what we were up to when things were halted can exist deep within the recesses of the sub conscience. We tend to want to 'finish' whatever the hell we were doing, and stop when *we* want to stop. This, however, is all just absolute nonsense. It is simply a knee jerk response that exhibits issues with authority among other things, and will serve no good purpose whatsoever.

The potential for this concept does not require you to remain unaware of these false intentions. This is largely due to the fact that they are often far *from* false. We will almost always have intentions of (at the very least) sampling our DOC, even knowing that the idea is to *not* engage in any drug activity. What must be done to ensure the success of this concept, is to make sure that you select any future reassessment 'dates' far enough ahead, that you have the chance to see through a good portion of the personal goals you are pursuing, thereby gaining some sense of accomplishment and self worth. If this is carried out as suggested, and each predetermined item of interest has been addressed (within reason), then the individual *should* have little problem selecting the proper path when the time comes. If doubt remains, give yourself another chance to get it right.

Although, if you do not feel this way and you do still want to go through with it, then please take certain factors into consideration before you do. First of all, you have been sober for however long now and so your tolerance is going to be non-existent. This makes for a situation where, should you relapse, you may tend not to realize that you must decrease the amount of opiates you ingest, so as not to overdose by flooding your detoxed system with unnecessary amounts of the drug. This is the way in which a large portion of people **die** as a result of opiate abuse, one of my best friends included. Please, play it safe and be very cautious. It will only take a fraction of what it once did to achieve the very same effect. Please keep a naloxone nasal pump on hand, and do not be afraid to use it if you think you might be falling out (overdosing). Nowadays many states are providing funding for these pumps to be handed out directly from the pharmacies free of charge, as they are quickly becoming the 'morning after' pill of the opiate world. Also, **always** make **sure** to have someone else nearby to keep an eye on you. If you are adamant about seeing this thing through, then please take every precaution necessary to avoid danger.

∞

It was just about two years ago now that I had been exposed to this type of scenario first hand yet once again. My best friend at the time, Jon, was on parole for a class B felony charge. While on parole Jon was living at a local sober home in Springfield, but spending a lot of time at his mom's house which was in a suburb of Springfield (and was near mine). Anyhow, he and I were pretty tight at this time, and when he began to dabble with opiates after remaining sober for just over a year or so, I was faced with the dilemma of how to help him to see the consequences of his actions. The problem being that, although I myself was drug free at the time, I was still very fresh in sobriety and not in any kind of shape to handle a situation such as this.

While I did attempt to steer him free of the drug and had offered to acquire some bupenorphine for him, he was insistent on staying this path to self-destruction in such a way that he would not be budged. Try as I did he just would not listen. And after pleading with him one Friday night to get back to the process of putting this all behind us, he declined any help, left my house and went and copped heroin from another addict right there in our own town. Jon then stopped at a local gas station to fix himself up. It being late evening by this time, this gave him the convenient cover of darkness to get high right there in his car (alone). I'm assuming he did what he always would, which was to dump about five bags in the 'cooker,' pull it *all* up into the syringe, and inject himself in the red ink portion of his (inside forearm) tattoo, in an effort to hide his tracks. As he did this, the drug had shown to be far stronger than that of what he had already been consuming, and, at twenty-seven years old Jon died right there in his car, at the gas station.

This was devastating on so many levels. Jon was just such a good guy that it really came as a great loss to many people. Just one year prior to this, Jon had been in jail for the first time and was waiting to be reunited with his family for the holidays (on parole). When his parole date was nearing and had reached only a few days away, the jail officials called him down to the counselors office and said that they had some news for him from home. I'm sure he was thinking what any inmate would have, that this was to be about his upcoming release and the details pertaining to such. When he arrived at the office, he saw that they had a superior officer there, as well as a woman from the forensics (mental health) unit, and finally a counselor, who had asked that Jon "please take a seat." They shut the door behind him, and it was then, he had told me, that he knew for sure something was definitely wrong.

Remembering that they had said this was news from home, he immediately felt a panic rising (as his mom and dad were both ill). The counselor then explained that the jail had received a phone call that morning from Jon's older brother, who had informed them that his father (who had been ill for some time now) had passed on over the night. The news had come only days before Christmas, and as devastating as this would be for anyone, Jon's ability to carry himself with complete composure was certainly noteworthy. I know that I personally would have been an absolute wreck. Jon, his mother (who was not well herself), and his slightly older brother, were now all alone on Christmas day left to pick up the pieces.

Jon's death came less than one year after that, and was a tragically sad event that had unfortunately occurred due to the fact that he had not taken into account the possibility of being sold bags that were made from a harmful batch of heroin. Whether it is an unusually strong batch, or a dangerously tainted batch (either by accident or *not*), one can never be entirely certain of the integrity regarding black market street drugs. Even if the 'stamp' or brand marking is one that is familiar, there will always be a chance of danger from tampering of some form. One can never know *when* they might be getting that extra strong batch, or a harmful, fake branding, and as a result it could all end just like that.

I really miss Jon. He was a funny little guy. He had done thirteen months in the county jail and came out with just one tattoo, it was a heart that said "I love Mom" inside it, and he had put it on his left butt cheek. Jon swore that it was his own idea and that he thought it would be funny. However, he *was* known to sometimes be a bit naïve, as well as being very trusting by nature. That being said, the joke very well may have been on him. The tattoo sure was.

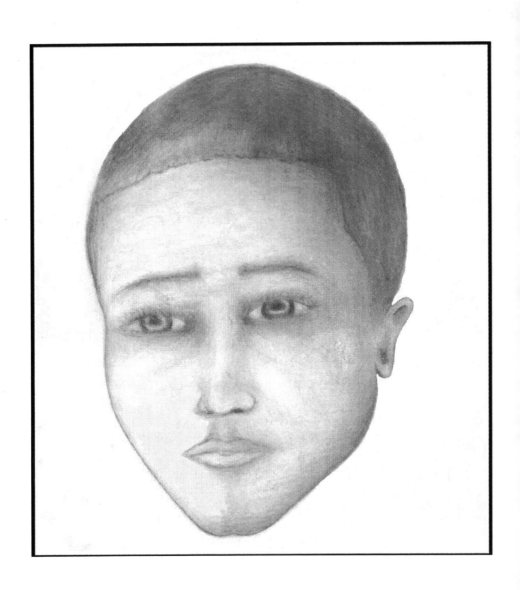

Considering Careers

I was beginning to come to the realization that this whole business of gaining a permanent position at the plant was just not going to happen. So I had begun to survey my options, as far as what I was going to do next.

For years now I had been hatching business plans and invention ideas, but before I could ever begin to see them through I would wind up falling off the wagon. I had made several attempts to come up with some type of career in which I would have the ability to provide relief for abused animals, as I *am* a proud animal rights supporter and have within me a strong desire to assist abused canines specifically. I would like to do more to help, but the type of help that I want to give requires funding which unfortunately I just do not have. For quite some time now I had seriously considered the success potential of a locally based residential program, modeled with the idea of tying two separate causes together (substance abuse and animal abuse). My thoughts, were focused on the positivity and assistance that could be achieved by opening a half-way house that would double as a canine rescue center.

This facility would have the two causes exist as one, where the residents would be trained to handle and work with the animals on a daily basis. These residents would then go on to each sponsor their own individual animal, as they each received the proper care and addressed whichever facets of their lives that may be in need of attention. I personally believe that this model could work quite well, if it were approached in the proper manner. I have observed other programs of a similar nature, and they seem to be making a difference. I personally think that a lot of good could be accomplished, as these damaged souls worked at healing life's wounds together.

However, the amount of political connections one needs to pull off such a thing right now, in this area anyhow, is just something I don't currently have. Still yet, the idea has potential if the proper circumstances were to arise. Like say for instance, if after this book were released I were to suddenly gain enough support for the idea, then perhaps something *could* be done with it. Only time will tell.

∞

Anyhow, I went about trying to come up with a plan that fit my situation. I had no capitol, no credit, and essentially nothing on paper that would suggest I was a feasible investment for *anyone* to get behind. I began looking to business models that required the bare minimum start-up cash. After considering a wide variety of scenarios, I had continuously returned to the idea of landscaping. I had previously been employed by a number of landscape companies and had gathered some real experience in the field. I enjoyed working outside, I was pretty good at it, and our area is perfect for it (everyone has big lawns around here). This was a business that required very little to get going, and could be performed by myself as *well* as my younger brother (who is disabled).

I had the labor aspect down pat. However, getting my hands on enough equipment to get *started*, was most assuredly going to be an issue. Not including the fact that I would then need to brush up on the business portion of owning such a company. It is one thing to do a couple of odd jobs here and there, but when you begin to experience true overhead costs, one learns quick the lessons of correctly quoting a job. Not only would it be a struggle just figuring out how to formulate price quotes, there would be a number of hardships to work through if I were to truly make this happen.

More importantly, there would be the task of seeking out and enticing customers who would be willing to give us a shot. I would also be faced with decisions when it came to selecting which distributors to work with in regards to lawn care products, etc. Soon there would be accounting issues to tackle, and of course making sure that I would be able to pay the bills while riding out the first, second, and probably third year that it will take to actually accumulate a profit margin wide enough that I'd be able to pay myself. Clearly I would have many obstacles to overcome, yet this plan continued to make the most sense. It was because of this that I had soon taken to honing my skills on the subject.

I went on YouTube and found that there are more than one video series out there that will walk you through *all* of these issues step by step. I began a routine of studying these videos on a daily basis, and had acquired a fair amount of knowledge regarding the field somewhat rapidly. I would also Google any and all questions I had had regarding this type of business, while taking thorough notes in the process. Before long I was networking with other guys who were already established in their own landscape businesses, and picking their brains as often as they would allow. You'll find that while in pursuit of your goals and upon reaching out for assistance, there are actually many people out there who are willing to go the extra effort and *help* in any way that might enable you to accomplish your ambitions (thankfully).

After some time I was making connections with various distributers and wholesalers, as well as equipment retailers and the like. Looking through Craigslist I had been able to locate just about every piece of equipment one would need to get started, for a fraction of the prices I was getting quoted from the dealers. However, the amount of cash it was going to take to purchase *all* of this stuff was still out of my range of possibility. So I would continue to research the topic and acquire price quotes for all of the *other* expenses that I would eventually incur, including but certainly not limited to, advertising and standard business overhead.

I can't say that I was altogether certain *how*, but it seemed I was determined to see this landscape thing play out. My mind just couldn't to let go of the idea.

The Search

After numerous attempts to get Burt on the phone with no luck, I had finally decided to go and check out his place and had my younger brother bring me over. Once we had gotten there, we could see clear into the living room and kitchen of his apartment through a little window in the top of his "front" door, and the whole place was entirely empty. Now, while I was led to believe that Burt didn't have a whole lot of stuff, he surely did have *some* stuff, and it was all gone. I commenced to banging on the door for a couple of minutes and was getting no answer back. I then figured I would take a ride over to the bar that Jerry (his landlord) had owned, to try and get some answers.

It was only about a five or ten minute drive and we were at the pub. I went in and immediately spotted Jerry behind the bar. This was a man who enjoyed living the rock star lifestyle and from what I could tell he had the rock star money to do it with. I'm not sure where he made his fortune or if his pub was just that successful, but his home, car, bar, everything was elaborate and top of the line. Jerry had shoulder length hair and dressed like he was an 80's pop metal star, always with at least one bandana tied *somewhere* on his body. Although it wasn't my kind of lifestyle, I respected it and found him to be a rather intelligent, decent guy. At first sight of him in there, I initially felt a brief feeling of hope rise within me. I couldn't help but sense that Jerry was going to be the key to unlocking this little mystery. I was sure that I would now be getting *some* kind of information.

Jerry recognized me right away and greeted me by offering a drink. I politely declined, and explained how I have a bad stomach that simply will not allow me to drink alcohol. He expressed his condolences to that fact as he slammed a shot of *Absolute* (something or other) himself, and went into a rant about Burt and something to do with sketchy passports.

Jerry had a good buzz on apparently, but he did make an effort to explain how Burt has for some unknown reason up and left the country. So now I want to know why, how, where, and huh? Out of the country? For what possible purpose could there be to make someone just flee the country with no warning whatsoever? Unfortunately Jerry was way too shitty to form a comprehendable sentence, which caused a bit of frustration on my part, and so I quickly traded numbers with him and got the hell out of there.

I went home and tried to go about my normal routine, assuming I would *somehow* find out something soon enough that would help to clear up this whole mess. Later that night I did get a text from a less inebriated Jerry, who apologized and said that Burt was involved in some kind of shady situation involving his passport. However, he couldn't give me any details to support this claim. He then informed me that Burt had in fact gone to Europe for, what Burt had described as 'personal reasons.' Jerry explained that one night Burt was there and everything seemed normal, the next morning he went to ask if Burt wanted to go out and grab some breakfast, and he was gone. Everything was gone. All of his belongings, his furniture. There was nothing left but a brief note for someone to please take ownership of his goldfish, Poseidon. Jerry informed me that he had no desire to care for a fish and if I wanted it, to let him know and he would get it to me.

So I texted Jerry to let me know when and if he heard anything else, and to go ahead and get Poseidon to me whenever he can. I then set about trying to piece together what the hell had happened to my buddy. Weeks passed by with no news. I was beginning to get really nervous and set about researching every little piece of info that I could find on Burt, but I was getting absolutely nowhere.

Was this to be the end of my time as Burt's "apprentice?" Perhaps this was all part of the 'plan' he had once spoke of, and I am to steer my *own* ship from this point further. Setting my own course for success and staying the path to enlightenment. Although, I had a hard time accepting the fact that he would just leave me high and dry like that, with no idea if he were alright or not. It just wasn't really his style.

Section Four Wrap Up

The individual who is pursuing these methods should now be reaching a stage where they are starting to feel healthier, inside and outside, mentally and physically. There should be a renewed sense of purpose beginning to rise within the subject, as well as an accompanied motivation unlike any other previously experienced. At this point, some of the key issues should be:

- An awareness regarding nutrition and how it relates to mood and physical comfort
- The understanding that there are herbal and nutritional supplements that *can* help in limitless ways
- Have an inside look into the criminal justice system and the war on drugs as it relates to the addict
- The desire to see some actual progress in the "war on drugs," being that we are victims of such
- Informed on Part Two of Burt's relapse hack
- Begin thinking on how you are going to go about earning a living (career) in this new life

Section Five

What's Next

I had mentioned previously that I am beginning the process of launching a grass roots non-profit organization that will aim to assist business minded individuals who are in recovery. I have pledged to donate a portion of every book I sell to the ASBSF (Association for Small Business Seed Funding), and I'm hoping that I will one day have what is needed to take this project to unprecedented levels of success. This organization will seek to provide small business start-up cash to individuals who have overcome personal struggles, including substance abuse and recidivism.

Qualified participants who have cleared a stringent interview process, as well as provided proper proof of rehabilitation, will then be selected to propose their idea. This involves another selection process, which if chosen, the participant will then take part in a preparation program put on *by* the ASBSF, as they await available funding.

At such time that funds do become available, select individuals will then be assisted with the various operations necessary when launching a new venture. The participant will agree to adhere to a set of rules set forth by the ASBSF, prior to the application process. Basically this is an agreement by the individual to pledge a predetermined fraction of future profits back into the ASBSF (in perpetuity), as a way of ensuring that there will be funds for the *next* success story.

I myself had dreams of ditching this drug habit of mine for my *own* business, as well as a sober successful life. However, after careful planning, months of research, and much effort put forth, I was entirely unable to secure financing of any sort. This, of course, was due to various factors, such as my sporadic employment history, a long criminal record, and very little of my own capital. These, are struggles that are experienced by entrepreneurs from all walks of life. Although, this should not take away from the fact that there are individuals out there with felony convictions and substance abuse histories who legitimately *do* have winning ideas, as well as the drive to see them through. In fact, they often possess a unique perspective that would benefit them greatly, were they *afforded* an opportunity to see their ideas play out. This is a result of the capacity to see the world from an angle that only we (as recovering addicts) can.

There is one other reason that I had made the choice to follow this cause. In the aftermath of every relapse I've ever endured, I would always be faced with same old mindset, that it was never going to matter how hard I tried, I'm just never going to be granted a loan or given a decent position in any kind of a career (as well as other negative thoughts of a similar nature). Now, although these types of issues are not going to be the case one hundred percent of the time, for someone of *my* status to succeed financially in any sort of reasonable time frame (in reference to my own situation), it would often feel just too challenging an idea to literally even dream about. I've always wanted the most out of life, and so from my perspective time was going to be of the essence.

I should clarify that not everyone desires the same kind of success. Some people are content just remaining sober while keeping a modest job and getting by with the bills. If this is enough for you that is terrific news, because this is actually a very attainable goal. It is an honest, humble lifestyle that I myself am for some reason unable to adhere to.

Had someone told me (during or after any one of my sentences) that I would be aptly compensated for my hard work and diligence, I would have almost certainly had a far better chance at beating this disease. While there are no guarantees when taking on an entrepreneurial venture, just an assurance that I would have been considered for a loan or assistance of some kind, purely based on the work in which I had put into it, the quality of the business plan, my ability to carry it out, and above all, without bias, this would have been the foot in the door that I had needed all along. Yet it had become pertinently clear that this was just never going to happen, understandably so.

So it has been my idea for quite a long time now to create an organization that would seek to provide for these needs, and attempt to utilize them as a sort of incentive program for those who are motivated and devoted to their rehabilitation. I can honestly say that if *I* were to have had an opportunity to receive assistance in any way similar to this back when I was in and out of jail, I would have devoted myself to putting together a solid business idea any way that I could in an effort to take advantage of the opportunity. It is my belief, drawing from ample experience, that there will surely be countless others out there who will show that they have what it takes to make things happen as well.

When I was bouncing back and forth from the streets, to programs, to jail, etc., I had learned how most lock-up institutions would control the inmate population within their facilities by using methods that are derived from those based on reward systems. This is how *I* have found the modern incarceration set-up to work, and from extensive research I've been able to verify that it is the norm mostly all across the country.

First, an inmate is placed into an isolated block of the institution for the first few days, pending various factors, including a Tuberculosis and sexually transmitted disease screening. After certain health concerns have been addressed and the individual is cleared by the medical department, they will then graduate to a larger section of the facility. This will be one which houses many inmates and is typically referred to as general population. Here there are more privileges as well as more freedom. This is where the facility tries to feel out each inmate individually, and get an idea of the amount of attention that each prisoner is going to require (especially if the inmate is to remain for a substantial period of time).

According to the individual's "classification" screening, they will then be afforded an opportunity to graduate yet once again. This next move is typically to a minimum or medium security unit, depending of course on whether or not the subject is classified as a low-risk to their community.

After that, the next step is out the door to a program, home, a half-way house, or perhaps (in some instances) an ankle monitor.

Each one of these phases carries with it more freedom and more privilege, but one false move and they will not hesitate to 'lug' the inmate right back behind the wall, where they would then be faced with having to start the process all over again. Although this type of set up does not work for *everyone*, I have observed the way in which the larger majority of inmates will take great pains to avoid losing these privileges, and it had gotten me thinking. If these men, who are often intelligent, capable adults who are full of potential and have simply lost their way, were to go to such lengths for a few minor amenities, then imagine what they might be capable of, were the amenities to carry a little more weight, say, the opportunity to launch their own company for instance. However, this program will not be for the ill equipped. Applying individuals are going to need to provide proof of utter devotion to their project, to their sobriety, and to this cause.

All of this weighed heavily on my mind over the last few years, and so I'm proud to say that I have now elected to go ahead and see my way through the process of starting this grass roots non-profit from scratch. I have extensive experience in dealing with individuals of this mindset, and I feel I can use my ability to communicate effectively as a way to aid in an individuals attempt to break free from this lifestyle. It is a worthy cause for *anyone* to support, and therefore I encourage any and all who sympathize to get involved. There will be no easy rides however, not for any of us. Just launching the program faces countless obstacles at every turn. If you want this program to assist you, it must succeed. Therefore if you want the program to succeed, then please get involved. I can not secure any kind of funding if the idea does not get the proper exposure it requires. Please, tell a friend to tell a friend to tell another. Take up the cause in your own unique way, and most of all get this book out there in any way you can! To those of you who think you might be eligible candidates and have thoroughly researched, well written business plans, please, come check it out.

Beechum's Bounty

During the time in between when my supervisor (Steve) had been informed of my meeting and the actual meeting itself, there were a lot of whispers around the water cooler regarding my situation. Everyone was well aware of my meeting, thanks to Steve's superb broadcasting abilities with even the most trivial of gossip. The talk was generally focused on whether or not I would be fired, and the vibe among them appeared to be predominantly toward the negative. Now, the other two gentlemen who were in line for the same position that I was after, easily joined onto the team of "haters," being that my leaving simply meant there would be one less obstacle for them.

Meanwhile (back at the ranch), it had been a few weeks now since I had last seen Burt. Though I had not spoken to *him* as of yet, I had finally tracked down enough info to at least know that he was OK. It was only a couple of days prior to this that I had received a call from Jerry stating that he had talked to Burt and had in fact confirmed that he did leave the country (briefly), and that he wanted a message passed to me explaining that he would be in touch soon. Apparently, he had lost his phone recently (which had all of his contacts in it) and he did not have my number written down. This was relieving news to hear, and had helped a little with the anxiety of my ongoing employment troubles.

So it was the night *before* the big meeting and I can not lie, I was scared to death that I might actually be losing my job. I started buying into the rumors and assumed that one of these guys had finally gotten their message through to corporate that they had wanted someone else to fill the position. I decided I would go online and do some research in regard to the landscape business, and maybe get my mind off of the meeting. When I went and logged on I saw that I had had a few emails, as usual, and so I began to sort through them. The first two were just nonsense (ads or something), but the *third* one was from a gentleman out of Spencer Massachusetts whose name was not familiar to me in the least. There was a brief note stating that he had something he wanted to discuss with me, and he had left a phone number for me to call "whenever I had some spare time."

I was intrigued by the tone in the note and had chosen to call right then. A gentleman answered on the second ring, and said "Lawn Story, how can I help you?" and I can remember thinking what on earth is this all about? I introduced myself, and he said that he was expecting my call. His name was Dominic, and he said that he had stumbled upon some of my correspondence with a few of the other landscapers online, and had taken an interest in the situation (regarding the fact that I was attempting to start a business as someone in recovery). Dominic said that he currently owned a large scale landscape company himself and has been very successful over the years. He also told me of how he has first hand experience dealing with substance abuse issues, regarding himself as well as several family and friends. Dominic said that he and some others close to him have all been freed from the obsession as well.

He then went into this big technical explanation, going into great detail about how his company has now gotten *too* big, and he has acquired several accounts reaching all the way to Western Mass where I live (he lived in Central Mass). He asked about my labor experience and then sort of quizzed me on some business related questions. These were some situational type questions like, "what would I do if *this* were to happen," and other similar scenarios. Apparently I had provided sufficient enough answers, because what he had to say next would become profoundly life changing for me. He explained, in a very matter of fact tone, that I could be taking on (assuming I were willing) all of his accounts from my area, all the way to a half-way point between he and I that he had apparently already determined. These would become my very own accounts, of which he wanted nothing in return, only the assurance that I would never let him or the customers down.

Dominic was an older gentleman who had achieved what he had set out to do with his life, and so he was now looking to use his good fortune in any way that could to assist a fellow sufferer get *their* chance at a better life. It was my determination to make use of the internet, getting my situation out there and tapping into the community of local business owners for any info that I could gather, that had led to what became a remarkably unique success story. Had I not done this simple task, my current lifestyle might have turned out considerably different.

Altogether it was thirteen solid accounts, with some part-time customers tacked on the end. This proposal of Dominic's would equate to an array of momentous opportunities for me. However, there *was* a catch. I would need to have all of the necessary equipment, as well as an insurance package with a fair amount of coverage, a work truck, a trailer, work orders, receipt books, business cards, and probably an employee or two. So, it would seem as though I were in a catch twenty-two of sorts. I could make myself some money if I had the equipment, but I needed a bit of money to get the equipment. This was certainly going to be an issue, as I didn't have *anything* to go on. Yet I was beginning to think that perhaps I could use the fact that I had some guaranteed work all lined up as a tool of leverage. It *was* possible that I might find someone to extend me a micro loan of sorts. I'll admit, it was a bit of a long shot, but I would give it a go anyhow.

The next morning I went to work dreading my impending meeting, but upbeat about the new developments with the business prospects. When had I pulled into the employee parking lot, Rob immediately rushed my car and "greeted" me as I got out to go punch in. He was all gitty and condescending with me this particular morning, and it was beginning to appear as though he had some kind of inside track on my disciplinary situation.

∞

By about two pm I was getting anxious and rather nervous. It had been an average day so far, aside from the (more than usual) sneers and jeers that I was getting from the 'cool kids.' Three o' clock (time of meeting) rolled up pretty quickly though, and it was time to go pay the piper. Steve called me over the radio (a hand-held unit that we each carried on the job) at 2:55, and he sounded as though he could hardly contain himself. He instructed me to head back to the shop, "it was time for my disciplinary meeting up in corporate." He said this over the radio nice and loud in an effort to demean me among my co-workers, but the majority of them couldn't stand him anyway.

I arrived at the shop at 2:59.

Steve gave me a snarl and said, "Your cuttin' it a little close don't you think?"

I said "Your absolutely right Steve, my apologies," which is not the response he was looking for I'm sure.

The two of us walked out of the shop and on to the corporate section of the facility. Now, when guys like us step foot up there in corporate, it just automatically feels awkward, primarily because we are wearing our work clothes. In other words, we are in uniforms that have seen a fair share of labor and show it. Everything up in corporate is spotless and expensive. There are baskets with free individually wrapped muffins, delicious looking danishes and pastries. Cold sandwiches are packed into a little refrigerator. There is fresh fruit, an iced coffee machine, as well as a separate cooler packed full with a variety of specialty beverages. Everyone is sporting the latest fashions, and one can be certain to overhear conversations about new BMW's, trips to the cabin, or "so and so just got accepted to such and such."

We came upon the desk of Mr. Beechum's secretary, Katherine. She was tall, very pretty, and sharp as a tack. All in all she was the talk of the campus as far as the opposite sex was concerned. She was young and ambitious, and had an ivy league education to boot. She stated that 'they' were expecting us and then advised us to have a seat, Frank would be out shortly. Now, did I just hear her say *they*? Steve could see my mind now spinning at the thought of some evil panel of professionals assembled for the sole purpose of firing *me*. Let's just say that he could tell I was nervous.

After five of the most awkwardly silent minutes of my life, Beechum opened the door and said "Who's Taylor?"

This would suggest that he didn't even know *who* Steve (the big shot) even was. If I know Steve, this must have hit him where it truly hurts, and yet there was still more to come.

So I said "I'm Taylor sir." And he instructed me to come on in.

As Steve gets up to escort me in, Beechum puts his hand up like a stop sign and says "Whoa big guy, where are you goin?"

"Well sir, I'm Mr. Taylor's supervisor and I just assumed," Steve replied as Beechum cut him off,

"Listen, pal, you know what they say about when one assumes..." he paused for effect while turning his gaze to Katherine, "you end up in the unemployment line Thursday morning!"

He said this with a smug chuckle afterward and I couldn't believe my ears. What the hell was going on here anyway? Steve was just completely deflated. His head sunk about as low as it could go, as he back-stepped his way out of the room without a word. So now *I'm* thinking, oh shit I'm screwed. If this is how they treat the employees that they like, then just what is it that they are going to do to *me*. And then I turned the corner into Beechum's office, to find Burt, Larry the Clown (as just Larry), and the doctor (Rosenberg) from the Albany hospital, all sitting there in Beechum's large office with a custom crystal whiskey bottle and some half-filled tumblers scattered about. They were all a buzz, and laughing at the expression on my face as I had rounded the corner and seen all of them together. Mr. Beechum closed the door, snickered to himself, and instructed me to have a seat and relax.

As I am grabbing a seat, Beechum grabs a file off his desk, comes around to the front of it and sort of leaned back against the edge. He was a rather sagacious, interestingly bland type of guy. While full of energy, clearly intelligent and unusually engaging, he was very general in his appearance. I likened him to that of the professor on *Gilligan's Island*.

"I assume you recognize at least one of these gentlemen here," he said while flipping through what I had thought was probably my employee file, and it was all I could do *not* to say "Well, you know what happens when you assume...," though I felt I was in no position to be making jokes.

I confirmed that I did know who everyone there was, as I turned to give Burt a "What the hell?" look.

245

Burt said, "Been lookin' for me have you bud?"

"Well yeah, you just up and disappeared." I replied.

"I understand," he said, "let's get through this meeting here, and then perhaps a little later on you and I can hang out so I can help to clear some things up."

I agreed, and then Beechum chimed in, "And are you familiar with Dr. Rosenburg or Larry here?"

"Yes sir I am, how are you guys?" I asked.

"Just fine. Burt and Frank here have had nothing but good things to say" the doctor replied.

Larry spoke up, "That look on your face as you turned the corner was something else," as he mimicked my expression with his jaw dropped exaggeratedly and his eyes bulging outward. He continued, "So I take it you had no idea at all *what* it was you were walking into."

"Not even close. I *thought* I was supposed to be here for a disciplinary meeting" I confessed. "Not to mention my surprise in finding that all of you guys seem to know each other!"

Beechum breaks in, "We have to be very careful in how we go about certain actions, and so I do apologize for leading you on in such a way."

"Oh, not at all." I assured him, though I had no idea *what* on earth he could of meant by that.

However, there had obviously been some type of theme revealing itself here, as the more I had come to know all of these guys, the more questions I would have.

The four of them then took turns speaking, while they explained to me how it was Mr. Beechum who had first spotted Burt and I out there on my break. He had said that he tried to catch us as he made his way out to the gate where we were at, but by the time he had gotten down there we were already

246

gone. Beechum then explained how, after seeing Burt, he was reminded of a mutual acquaintance of theirs, Dr. Rosenburg. So he then phoned the doctor, who informed him that Burt and he *had* in fact been in contact as of just recently, though he had not been able to reach him on his cell phone for a couple of weeks now. He said that he did, however, have the number of another mutual friend of theirs (who I never did get the name of) and gave Beechum the information.

Mr. Beechum then made some more calls, and after a bit of effort was able to track Burt down. When he did finally reach him, they of course got caught up on current affairs first off. The conversation would soon take a turn toward myself however, and all that had been transpiring on and off the job there at the plant. Burt laid it all out regarding Steve, Rob, the other temps, and all the childish nonsense that I had been putting up with. They then talked about all of the success that I had experienced thus far in terms of recovery. Burt went on to inform Mr. Beechum of my desire to launch my own landscape/lawn maintenance company, as well as all of the work I had done to prepare myself for just such a thing.

"The first order of business here, would be the issues you have been having with a couple of my regular employees. Who is it, Steven Cardona and Robert O'Neill? Now, tell me in your own words just what it is that has been going on" Mr. Beechum instructed me.

I began to tell a story that focused on the fact that all I've wanted since I had started there, was to obtain a full time permanent position that would enable me to provide for my family. I explained that I had truly loved working there and had pushed my physical limits as I tried to impress my superiors with quality, efficient work. Although it was through this process that I had perhaps shined a little *too* bright, and created a few adversaries as a result. I told Mr. Beechum that I only meant to secure a position and wished no ill will toward anyone.

Before I could continue on any further, Beechum says "Whoa, whoa, slow down, let me ask you something," as he holds up a finger, putting the conversation on pause while he speaks into the intercom portion of his desk phone. "Katherine, can you please locate two employee files? One is Steven Cardona first shift maintenance, and the other is Robert O'Neill third shift

247

maintenance, thank you."

The secretary acknowledged his request and he then turned his attention back to me and continued.

"Now, tell me this," as he is rummaging through his desk for something, "where do you feel most comfortable working in this plant?"

"Well sir, I enjoy the job I *have* quite honestly (which was in the maintenance department). Although it has been a little difficult as of lately, enjoying it as I once had that is" I responded.

"I'm well apprised of that situation and we are going to address that momentarily" he said as he finally located a brand new box of golf balls from the back of a desk drawer. He's now got a pile of junk from all of his drawers spread out over the top of the desk, which he is sorting through as he is carrying on the conversation.

Just then, the secretary knocked, entered the room and placed two file folders on his desk.

She said smiling, "Oh, I can see your making a mess as usual," which drew a roar from the room, "anyhow, here are the employee files you requested sir, and just a reminder you've got a 5:30 tee off time at *Cedar Knob* this evening."

He thanked her and said that that would be all for now. After we all watched as Katherine sauntered her way out of the room, we then sat through a few minutes of silence while Beechum skimmed through the two files, muttering pieces of sentences as he read to himself. I turned to look at Burt, who just made a face back and held up his hands as if to be saying, "I don't know what's going on either." It was clear, however, that he had to know more than *I* did at this point.

As Mr. Beechum was finishing up looking over the files, he asks, "Now are these two gentlemen pulling this type of shit with any of my other employees?"

"Not that I have witnessed sir." I replied.

"Uh-huh, uh-huh. OK, so let me ask you this, what have you got right now for landscape equipment?"

I can only presume he's making idle chit-chat here, why on earth he would be concerned with any of *that.* It was clear that I had no idea *what* was going on. So I explained how I really didn't have anything other than know-how, ambition, motivation, and thirteen solid accounts to work on.

He looked at Burt when I mentioned the new developments and said, "Did you know about this?" and Burt, looking a bit surprised himself, said "No, not at all. This is certainly something that happens to coincide quite nicely with what we're doing here." I'm still in the dark here as to *what* it is they're talking about.

Burt makes a nodding gesture for me to turn my attention back to Beechum, who begins to ask me some of the details regarding these accounts. After I laid it all out for him, he explained to me that the four of them had gotten together in an effort to assist me in my quest for success. Beechum then told me how the plant had had their own industrial lawn maintenance equipment, which they had purchased just a year or two ago. This was an idea that had never really played out as well as they had hoped. It was supposed to save the company some money, though for some reason or another they continued to have problems sorting out who would take on the position (this was long before I had gotten there). So they continued hiring landscape companies for temporary periods of time, and were effectively losing even more money. Finally, they signed a contract with an outside firm to handle everything from that point on and never looked back. They are now contractually obligated to use the services of this particular company for a period of no less than five years.

"We've got everything out there, a rider (mower), a walk-behind, a trailer, backpacks (blowers), weed whackers, and a ton of extra stuff along with it all" Beechum informed me.

"So here it is," he said. "Would you prefer it if you were to be given a permanent position doing what you do here now," pausing briefly before continuing on, and I wanted to shake my head yes already.

I was of course sold on this idea, yet he still had more to say.

"Or, would you like to take all of that equipment out there and have a go at your own business?"

Holy shit! Is he serious? Throughout my entire life I had not had very many positive things like this happen for me, and now I'm getting good news from all directions. This was just too unbelievable. As hard as I was trying to hold back from showing *too* much emotion, one lone tear squeezed it's way out of my eye and slowly rolled to the tip of my nose. Embarrassed, I wiped it away quickly and composed myself enough to respond with an enthusiastically grateful "Hell yes I'll use the equipment!" They all begin to chuckle over my excitement, and commenced to chiming in with things like "Good for you!" and "Atta boy!"

Mr. Beechum then asks about Steve and Rob, and whether or not I thought there should be some kind of punitive measures for them. This sounded a bit extreme to me and I simply explained that I held no animosity toward anyone there. I wouldn't want anything to interrupt their ability to feed their families (certainly not like they were trying to do to me). I explained how, if it were up to me, he never would have even heard about the whole mess. To which he reminded me that, had I not spoken up, things would never have panned out the way that they had. Still, I thanked him for the gesture but asked that he just let that be.

"Well sir, I suppose I can respect that decision" said Beechum, "Anyhow, did you see Steve's face just then when I was screwing with him back there?" "I'll bet you when he got back to the shop he laid into *somebody* for no good reason" Beechum added, with one eye on the clock and one on the door.

And at this, the rest of the room broke into a brief laughter.

Mr. Beechum then stood up, and as he did everyone else began to stand up as well. He explained that he had a tee off time approaching, but that he and I would meet very soon. He said to just keep doing what I was doing for now, he would call me up to his office sometime the following day. We all shook hands, well, *I* shook hands. They all shook each others forearms, for some reason which I had yet to figure out. We then all filed out of the office and straight into corporate. Mr. Beechum bid his secretary good night, which spawned numerous good nights from the entire group, and then he walked with us while carrying on a conversation with the doctor about various golf courses. Burt and I had made some quick plans to meet up that night (though we wound up meeting the following day), and we all parted ways. I would now commence to processing everything that had transpired over the last couple of days. I was all in now, set to experience a quality of life of which I had never known before.

Sleep Tighter

When one begins to sink back below the clouds and starts to regain some sense of reality, one of the first plans of action should be to address any existing health problems. The individual must also get thoroughly examined for any possible *unknown* conditions. There are thousands of ailments that you very well may have contracted and not even know it. When we are subjected to places such as detox units, residential treatments, correctional institutions, shooting galleries, etc., we put ourselves at high risk for numerous highly contagious conditions.

Often these types of ailments affect all sorts of areas, and so it is especially important that you ask your physician to examine certain areas with extra caution, including but not limited to: skin, scalp, lungs, immune system, genital area, and blood. There are so many easily transmitted conditions that have the ability to affect a startlingly vast number of areas regarding your health, body, mood, appetite, sex drive, sleep patterns, teeth/gums, and again, this list could go on and on as well, but you should get the idea by now.

∞

If you have led a life anything close to my own, then you too have most certainly gone through numerous sporadic sleep patterns as well. This is a key area of interest during this phase, and if it is not addressed properly, it can affect your mood, physical health, and most importantly - your chances at quality sobriety. You should start working on a daily sleep schedule that follows the same as you would if you were employed. This will help when first stepping out to gain employment or seek further education, as you will already be accustomed to the routine of getting up early, as well as getting to bed at a reasonable hour. Your general health will improve by doing so, effectively making you look and feel better all around.

Starbuck's Park

I had arranged to meet up with Burt at about 2pm the day after the meeting. We of course met up at the same coffee shop we had *always* gone to, and this was what I had thought was going to be a chance to try and pick up where we had left off. I was also under the impression that Burt was going to fill me in on just what it was that had been going on with him, with regard to his sudden disappearance (among other things). However, things do not always pan out exactly the way you envision them.

For once, *I* was the first to show up at Starbucks, which I'll admit did make me a tad nervous. Though Burt did arrive soon after, and without a word went straight to ordering his usual, a medium black hazelnut. Aah, just like old times. Everything was beginning to feel right with the world again. Yet when Burt sat down, I could see in his expression that there was another change coming. With all that had been going on, I had failed to account for the fact that Burt had his own problems. I, of course, would want to do anything I could to help, though I never could tell if he was going to let on what the trouble had been or not.

Anyhow, I began inquiring about the passports, Europe, and his apartment at Jerry's, and Burt was unexpectedly forthcoming with the details. He explained, first of all, how Jerry had misinterpreted the whole situation with the passports. Burt had simply grabbed an old expired one by mistake, and when he was at the airport, he needed to have a friend call in a favor so that he could still fly without having to rush back home.

I next asked about Europe, and it was clear that he was getting emotional at the very mention of it. It didn't take long to understand why. What he had to say was both shocking and sad. He explained how he had once lived in a somewhat small town in England, along with a wife and two step-children. He then said that he and the wife (Dianne) had separated long ago, but on unusually good terms. Unfortunately, Dianne had become very ill some time back, and so he now tried to do whatever he could to be a source of support for her. They had been in consistent contact, a bit more often lately with the illness progressing, and so she had clearly looked to draw on Burt for emotional and spiritual support (albeit from across the ocean).

Burt continued on, and said that it was about *five* weeks back now that he had received a devastating phone call one morning, just as he was heading out the door to meet up with a friend. It was a physician over in London, England whom Burt was familiar with, and, after exchanging hello's the doctor informed him that he was unfortunately calling with terribly tragic news. The doctor admitted, sadly, that he was reaching out to inform him that his (Burt's) step-daughter, Abby, had been killed in a car accident just the night before. As if this weren't terrible enough, the doctor also had then said that Abby's mother (Burt's ex-wife), being ill already, was hospitalized after the news had thrown her into a deep, dark depression, to the point that she'd (for all *practicle* purposes) gone near mute.

All of this came as a great shock of course. The young girl had just turned sixteen and was destined for big things. She was an honor student, captain of her field hockey team, and an avid pianist (which Burt had taught her as a small child). Abby made a mistake and got into the wrong vehicle for a ride home after leaving a friends house that previous evening. The driver (a fellow classmate) was intoxicated far beyond legal limits, for what was actually his first time ever, and swerved into oncoming traffic, killing himself, Abby, and another female schoolmate.

Burt was reeling from the news and felt completely helpless, as anyone would. Without a word to Jerry (or anyone) he packed his belongings and put them in storage, bought a plane ticket online, and left for England. Once there, he made some quick lodging arrangements, and went straight to helping get Dianne through this awful event. He tended to Dianne, while at the same time handling all of the necessary arrangements. Burt paid for all of the funeral and burial expenses, and had a very elaborate headstone carved, with the shape of a *Baby Grand* piano sitting atop the stone. Abby had always dreamed of one day owning such an instrument, and I guess Burt felt this was his last chance to give her one. I believe he wanted to give his step-daughter a top notch send off and show that he still cared for her, as well as her mother and sister.

The whole situation had sparked many emotions among Burt and the family. He and Dianne found that they now needed each other more than ever. Not only this, but the other daughter (Pria), was now left with a massive void after surviving two of her mom's failed relationships, and now losing her sister whom she was extremely close with. The two sisters had learned to lean on each other over the years, which created a bond that was unlike any other. Pria would now need a sound family structure in order to come out of this situation with a stable frame of mind.

Anyhow, they all came to realize that they would now need to remove one bothersome element *to* their situation, the Atlantic ocean. They talked and talked about it, and decided that it would be best if Burt were to move back to the UK. I agreed, it just seemed to make perfect sense. Burt said that he had some affairs that he must to attend to before going back, one of which being myself and my own ongoing saga. I reminded him that his situation required his attention far more so than my own. I explained that he had done so much already, but he stopped me mid-sentence and insisted that there were a few things in particular that *must* be discussed now.

We would always meet at this particular Starbucks because there is a quiet little park right nearby. Sometimes we'd get our coffee and then go over there to sit, so that Burt could talk without being disrupted. It was a nice day out, and so this is what we chose to do just now. We grabbed fresh coffees and made our way over to the park where we came upon this massive old fallen tree. This particular tree had protruded from the ground in such a way that it made a perfect spot for people to sit and enjoy the park. Fortunately for us the tree was available and so we had a seat.

Burt began by commending me for handling everything as best as I could. He also gave me a sort of "congrats" about the landscaping gig, and as he was talking he reached down and picked up an average sized stick from the ground. I watched as he pulled out this little pocket knife that he had always carried with him, opened it up, and began to carve away at the wood. He had once told me a story of how his father had given this knife to him, just before walking out the door to 'find work,' never to return and leaving Burt and his mother to fend for themselves at a time when survival was on a day to day basis. As he talked, he whittled away at this stick, and I sat in complete captivation as he began projecting an interesting hypothetical scenario. It was apparent right away that he was depicting what could become the very essence of what my life will and shall be from that point on.

He incited butterflies in my stomach as he talked about a not so distant future, one where I am of a substantially more comfortable financial status. He then described what it could be like once I learn just how to embrace this new found importance. My thoughts and opinions will soon carry a little more weight with those around me, perhaps a bit more often than I had been accustomed to. He wanted me to understand the importance in securing some property, a home, and to focus on small business expansion as well. Burt was able to give me a boost by shedding light on a handful of attributes that I had attained without really even noticing, and which are going to be necessary in owning and running any business. He had also made note of a couple areas which could stand to use some work, from my learning how to better manage my obsessive compulsive behaviors and turn them to my advantage, all the way to my need to rise above my vague understanding of general politics and small business tax laws. Understand that these areas of interest are specific to my situation, and will not always be the same as your own.

Burt said that I must now buckle down and "take the reigns" so to speak. He informed me that I've only begun to scratch the surface of my capabilities, and that I should always be at the ready to explore them whenever they reveal themselves. He began to roll up his sleeve as he was finishing his sentence, and when he did so he unveiled to me the tattoo that I had once caught site of a couple of years prior. It turned out that I had been right, I *had* seen the image before. It was the shape that I had woken up to draw in the middle of that night not so long ago, after recognizing the shape in an unusual (otherworldly) dream. Yet there was one other instance in which I had crossed paths with this shape.

It was at a company picnic I had attended while working at the plant part-time a couple of years back. Frank Beechum was out there playing volleyball with some of the 'common folks' from the manufacturing department, and I was on the other team. Anyhow, Beechum was wearing a tee shirt, for the first time that I had ever been witness to, and I had remembered taking notice of his tattoo. His was also on the *right inside forearm*, and I was just then finding out that it was near identical to Burt's.

Burt then informed me that this shape was actually something which "they" referred to, as the *Parazod*. This seven sectioned figure was deeply symbolic, representing the seven stages of transmutation first and foremost. This Parazod is known to generally consist of three main colors, yellow, red, and blue, each one of certain alchemical importance (or this is how it was interpreted anyway). I should add that I have learned how it *has* also been known to sometimes incorporate other colors, such as green, purple, or orange, but not typically. The shape itself was known to be of use in different fashions for different reasons. I was told how the figure was discovered long ago, and was said to exist as a tool and focal point in at least two known civilizations, one of Peruvian decent and the other of Manchurion (or something like that). According to Burt these discoveries were made near simultaneously, and the symbol was thought to be utilized and revered in an almost identical manner across both civilizations (spanning centuries as well as oceans apart). Burt said that the varying points between them were actually too irrelevant to even mention. However, I also think that he was trying not to bog me down with information that was not as important at that time, as there *was* a lot to take in.

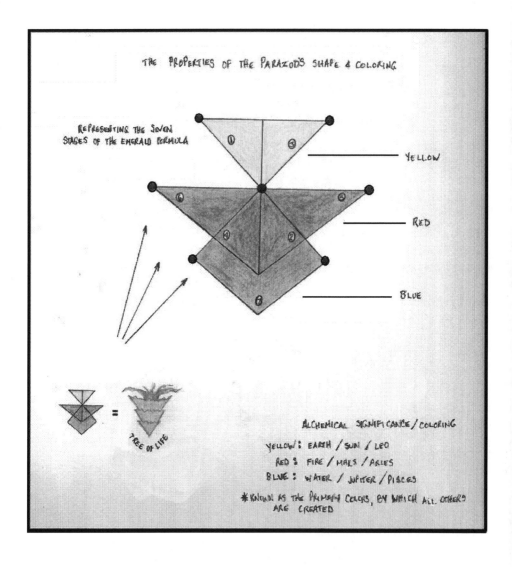

THE PROPERTIES OF THE PARAZOD'S SHAPE & COLORING

REPRESENTING THE SEVEN STAGES OF THE EMERALD FORMULA

YELLOW

RED

BLUE

TREE OF LIFE

ALCHEMICAL SIGNIFICANCE / COLORING

YELLOW: EARTH / SUN / LEO
RED: FIRE / MARS / ARIES
BLUE: WATER / JUPITER / PISCES

*KNOWN AS THE PRIMARY COLORS, BY WHICH ALL OTHERS ARE CREATED

The tattoo, which depicted this Parazod, I've been told was a symbol among *certain* men who at one time were all very active in attempting to unravel the intricate design of our universe. They did this as part of an effort to elevate themselves and their fellow mankind to 'that of an enlightened state.' It was purely coincidental, I found out, how my boss had also in some way been part of this as well as Burt. The way Burt had once described it,

"Most will go there entire lives without ever having *knowledge* of crossing paths with one of [his] 'brothers,' and here you have stumbled into two at once" This is reflective of one of the main focal points of my little story here, which is that it would appear as though I have had my life drastically altered by extreme coincidence many times over now.

Anyway, Burt explained to me how they (he and his *colleagues)* had developed a theory of sorts, after many years of observing trends, percentages and the like. They had taken extra notice of crime statistics, prison populations, current drug trends, foreign drug trends (and laws), as well as the economic impact of all of these issues. He said that what they had found, is that our society is drastically affected simply by what drugs are "popular" at that time. They then found that the drug trends could therefore have the ability to economically impact a weakened economy. These men learned that, when compared to any other, heroin affects the world in a way that is yet to be matched. It has now been established, that a country in the grips of a heroin 'epidemic' can suddenly find itself in the need of numerous services. These services, henceforth, create the need for many employment opportunities throughout a vast number of fields, including detoxes, med clinics, therapists, pharmaceuticals, ER unit physicians and nurses, EMT's, residential treatment centers, and (depending on who you ask) prisons, correctional workers, police, DEA, FDA, FBI, ATF, CIA, task forces, detectives, etc.

So anyhow, Burt then went on to tell me how many of these men were, and are of rather importance in their communities, and will not support any idea that could possibly incite theories of conspiracy. In fact doing so was looked upon unfavorably by their peers, and so therefore any time the data pointed *towards* such a thing, they would go to great lengths to disprove it. Burt said that they had been trying to understand the logic surrounding the way in which our country has handled the increasingly dangerous opiate/drug abuse for many years (as well as a means of correcting the situation), and have in fact partially disbanded as a result of ongoing arguments *regarding* the matter.

Back when this research (and turmoil) was well under way, Burt had decided to branch off from the friction occurring among the group, and turn his perspective toward a different direction altogether. It was when *his* data had begun to show some actual possibilities, that a few of the other gentlemen involved had started to take him seriously. What Burt and these gentlemen were looking into, was whether or not an addict who is recovering after any kind of lengthy opiate "bender," could possibly be more apt to respond to efforts of transmutation (by way of educational, inspirational, emotional, and motivational stimuli), any more so than the average individual (*not* in recovery).

The results, Burt stated, had been blatantly one sided. He said there was no question that the addict in recovery *is* in fact more likely to show response to these and other types of stimulation. He explained how this is partially due to the way in which we as addicts tend to keep ourselves focused on a few simple objectives for such long periods of time. When the time finally comes and we sober up, we will *typically* abandon all previous reservations and soon find ourselves rediscovering life (and our world) as we embark on a journey into recovery.

Burt explained how this process just happens to leave the individual in precisely the proper state of mind and spiritual receptiveness, that the whole experience of being 'strung out' on opiates and then subsequently detoxing and becoming sober, can literally render the individual enhanced, with a refreshed capacity to be altered for the better. This, he explained, is not unlike the receptiveness of that of a child, passionately eager to learn and experience life. He reminded me how many of the actions necessary are small variations of principles that are already routinely practiced by the typical recovering addict.

He then pulled out a file folder and handed it to me and I had immediately recognized it as being the very same file that Dr. Rosenberg had given to *him*, way back when we had taken the trip to Albany. He began talking me through the seven steps of the Emerald Formula and the variations with which he had been experimenting with thus far, as I flipped through the folder packed with equations and alchemical writings of all sort. He was giving me a crash course in his own interpretation of an alchemical process that had been producing, what Burt had regarded to be, actual positive results. We discussed each stage to great extent and its importance as it relates to the addict.

Burt then told me quite a bit more regarding the Parazod and the other men involved. He gave an in depth history of the group, but never revealed to me any kind of a name or moniker for them. I have been researching this ultra secretive order of modern day philosophers ever since, but what little I *have* found has come at a slow pace. He went on to tell stories of wealth and fortune, power struggles, and how he had chosen to break off into his own direction, which had created issues of envy among certain men as a result. As he was carrying on, he continued whittling away at the stick and it just continued to get smaller. I had begun to wonder whether or not he was trying to make something or just shave it down to a nub.

Continuing on, Burt said that although I *had* come a long way, there was still much work to be done. He insisted that I would need to continue to improve on my self respect first and foremost. He then said that I needed to seize this opportunity while it exists, and began inquiring as to whether or not I had realized the obstacles that still lay ahead of me. He expressed the importance in my understanding and acknowledging the magnitude of the amount of energy that will be required, if I expect to achieve any kind of *real* progress.

I was informed that I was not randomly selected for this task, "If you aren't sure, then let me tell you, you have something unique that is beneficial to *your* community of like minded individuals, and this is the reason for which you are here now," he stated.

Burt then continued, "I have put an immense amount of effort into seeing you through this, because I honestly feel that there is something within you which desires to see your fellow man succeed and prosper. You must continue to make a success out of me *and* yourself, by inspiring future success stories with what you have learned."

I began to feel as though I were in one of those kung fu movies that I love so much, with Burt as the Abbot (or master monk), warning me not to use my kung fu for evil and that sort of thing. Anyway, Burt then explained how he was going to be returning to the UK soon, and that there was a possibility that he could remain there indefinitely. He was shaken by these recent events so much so, to the point that mortality had suddenly scared up a renewed sense of family and the overwhelming need to be with them. He explained how he had planned on working with me for quite a bit longer than this, but that fate had yanked his soul "back across the pond," and he figured he might as well go join it.

I continued to watch as he started to use another attachment on his pocket knife, working the center of the stick and appearing to hollow it out (like a tube). He said that he felt as though what we've accomplished so far, everything that he has taught me, and all that we had been covering here today was plenty enough for me to make good use of for quite a while. I was instructed to find a way to use what I now know as a means of helping out as many other sufferers as I can. He said that we as adults, here living in this time, are some of the last true defenders of man's ability to think for himself. Burt warned me not to put any unwanted emphasis on a man's past or where he's been, but rather where he can *go*.

"And then give him the directions on how to get there" he added.

Burt also wanted me to know that I shouldn't ever let myself or another become overwhelmed concerning alchemical details. He said that if these theories ever become the focus, more so than the *recovery*, then it's time to fall back and regain some sense of the results and not so much the ideas behind the methods used to achieve them. It will serve no purpose (for the addict seeking recovery) to become obfuscated by confusing theories and terminologies.

Finishing up his carving, he dusted it off, blew it out, and then held it up to his lips. With two fingers placed over two little holes which he had driven through the top of it, he then began to blow into it softly with his fingers lightly fluttering. As he did this, a sweet, melodic pan flute'ish sort of sound came chirping out, and it had taken only a minute or so before Burt had found just the right way in which to use it. Thirty seconds or so later two little songbirds came swooping down from a big nearby tree and perched side by side on a branch of a rhododendron bush that was a little ways to the right of where we sat. They too began chirping away and it was amusing too see Burt now begin to go back and forth with them.

"Turtle Doves," he whispered. "I spotted them when we got here. That slightly larger one there is the male, and the other, I would imagine, is his lady friend."

He handed me the carving and said that if I were to ever come back to that same spot again, to bring some sunflower seeds.

"They go crazy over them" he said, as he scratched his head and looked at his watch.

Now, any time in the past when Burt and I would go to part ways, we would just say something along the lines of 'see ya,' or 'talk to you later.' However, this particular occasion Burt had done something a bit different than usual, he raised his hand to shake mine. So I reached over, grabbed his forearm and shook as he let out a chuckle.

Idle Hands, Off

Upon that point at which you have now made a fair effort to structure your time, you may very well still be faced with various periods throughout the day where you find yourself idle. There is a mountain of work to be done of course, though not every task can be carried out at your convenience. Therefore, certain actions will surely be put off until such time as they can be completed.

This type of scenario occurs in all of our lives, and it tends to leave gaps of idle time throughout our schedules (assuming that the individual is unemployed and has not yet reached that stage). These are the times that we as addicts must pay the closest attention to, as many will find it is the most commonly susceptible time for relapsing. Although we all must take some breaks for rest, it is important to understand what an acceptable amount of time for rest is. As adults we generally know when we *should* be doing something, and so this area can really be based on your own good judgment. Yet if an individual is finding themselves with an ample amount of free time, then some aspect of their recovery is clearly in need of attention.

Any individual that is in recovery is clearly in no position to "kick back" and relax. That is to say, one needn't relax any more than enough to rest the body and the mind. There is so much to do on a daily basis that demands our constant vigilance, that spare time *should* be just about non-existent. If you want success all around like I do, then you are going to have to work at it 24/7. There are many areas of interest that one can look to when they are finding themselves unsure of what to do. It's OK, this happens to everyone at one time or another. The difference of course lies in how we each deal with it.

A renewed successful life will demand that the individual be constantly accountable and responsible. So, carrying one's self as such on a daily basis will surely help to better prepare them for handling different situations as they arise. The way we do this is by beginning to take *everything* seriously. No matter what it is you are doing, it will serve you best to treat the task as though your are 'on the job.' In other words, it would be in your best interest to approach this whole process of recovery as though it were your new employment position. Whatever it is that needs to be done to change your life, be it addressing health concerns, improving on appearances, educating ourselves, or exercising the concepts throughout this text, take some pride in each and every single task (however uneventful).

The individual who has been following the concepts in this text, by this point, *should* now have the desire to start working at creating a spotless, clean cut, organized, and orderly image. This can be accomplished first of all by staying busy with tending to whichever areas of your life that may be in need of 'polishing.' Perhaps your home, apartment, border room, jail cell, etc. could use some deep cleaning as a way of ridding one's life of the dirty grime of the past. Or maybe your car is in disarray and in need of attention. Others will find that their wardrobe needs updating, and so using resources such as the Salvation Army, et al. will be necessary. Even if the subject has zero resources at the moment, one could still try washing and mending some of their existing belongings, giving old tattered things a refreshing new appearance.

I feel it is a natural human inclination to want to feel clean and organized. I also feel that when a person is *not* clean and organized, they are in turn left feeling a bit off. As for myself, I know that I feel better, as well as sleep much more comfortably, when myself and everything around me is linen fresh and neat. The organized piece to it is simple, if the physical world is in disarray, the mental aspect of it has got to follow suit to some extent.

Organization of one's life often seems like a chore initially, although aside from the obvious benefits, it *can* also become your first line of defense against relapse. This logic here is simple, following a well thought out schedule each day and not allowing ourselves to be compromised, will no doubt help to steer us from any possible threatening situations.

An an individual who is piecing together a broken life will most assuredly have numerous medical appointments, therapy sessions, as well as a number of other personal engagements with which there will be a considerable amount of effort needed to arrange and keep track of. This is **very** important to understand. Keep all of your appointments, no matter how minor they may appear to be. When we begin allowing ourselves to miss appointments of *any* sort, for no legitimate reason, what happens is we gradually slide further and further into a rut. Creating a situation where (ultimately) we feel we have now let so much go, that there is just no coming back from it. This occurs due to the fact that the individual would now be faced with the problem of keeping up with current engagements, while simultaneously making up for missed ones. The recovering addict tends to deal with these types of scenarios especially poorly, and then of course what happens is the disease wins yet again.

The focus of this principle throughout, is to be constantly working toward a better today as well as a better tomorrow. Although yesterday will resonate forever in video, audio, the written word, and in our minds, it needn't be bothered with by the recovering addict.

Pick up Six (and seven)

As I have mentioned a couple of times now, this book was originally put together as seven sections. However, after I began formatting and entering the information into an e-book program, I realized that I was going to face some size constraints. I was going to have to either shave the book down, or do what I ultimately elected to do, which was to split off the final two sections and create for them a book of their own.

The first five sections contain within them the very same essential methods and principles involved in the process that I had gone through. There is enough to do concerning the "first five," that an individual pursuing this type of path will need to reach a certain level of achievement before attempting to tackle the remaining two sections. These final two sections delve into making quality use of the work that the individual has put forth throughout the first five. In fact, there is enough information regarding these last two sections, that the size restrictions I had experienced with the first book had soon threatened to affect the second as well.

Section six and seven will help to steer the individual toward a path of education, employment, re-establishing connections with family and friends, relationships, small business, politics (advanced), big business (advanced), and the development of an investment portfolio (advanced) among many other important topics. These final two sections are where the real thinking man's work begins. One can make excellent use of these tools and go on to enjoy an unlimited level of success, **provided** that the first five have been followed diligently for an adequate amount of time.

There is also a piece on what direction to go with the medicinal treatment aspect, once a certain level of achievement has occurred. The individual should seek to begin a weening down, and perhaps off of the bupenorphine or methadone. However, if you don't feel comfortable just yet dropping your dose, but feel your ready to move forward with other actions, this too is OK. Some people find that they need anywhere from six months to three years to five years, to perhaps even permanent daily medication. This should not be frowned upon or avoided, *if* it is what the individual requires in order to remain drug free. Many have learned that the bupenorphine/methadone provides the pain relief that they had needed all along, in a safe and controlled manner.

As I had spoken about in previous chapters, it is likely that there was an underlying condition which had helped to nudge you toward opiate relief in the first place. Many of us will notice that our individual systems were so rapidly receptive to the opiates (possibly more so than others), due to the body's yearn to be rid of these symptoms that had been brought on by whichever ailments might have existed. In this scenario, I would suggest that the individual find the lowest possible dose that still provides adequate relief, and then work on maintaining that dose while continuing on working through the stages.

This is the End

It had been a few months since Burt had returned to the UK, and things were well under way with the landscape business. My brother and I were steadily busy tending to all of these new accounts. I was working on a plan to try and arrange *something* with Mr. Beechum, to allow me to remain at the plant long enough that I would be able to earn what I had needed to purchase a work truck, insurance coverage, and some other odds and ends (small hand equipment, etc.). But I was once again met with yet another surprise.

When I finally had gotten an opportunity to approach Beechum about this idea, he said that he was already well aware that this was an issue for me, and then began to cut me a personal check right there on the spot.

He said, "Give me a realistic figure on what it is you must have to get this thing going."

He informed me that this was a personal loan from him to me, and that I did not need to stress about paying it back anytime soon.

"For what little you actually need, I can't see putting this thing off any longer. You've got fall clean-ups coming soon, and what's going to happen is you are going to wind up *losing* money."

After pretending to do some quick math in my head, I gave him a number of which I had already calculated (approximately) numerous times over at home, and he didn't even blink. Without skipping a beat, Beechum wrote in the amount, we shook forearms (I was getting good at this now, even when they weren't expecting it), and I was on my way as a true business owner.

My brother and I had worked hard all of that summer and fall, and it was during our off time over the winter that I had put forth the effort necessary to begin creating this book. This had been a huge learning experience, as the knowledge I have gained I'm sure will prove to be beneficial to me in the long run.

273

I have since repaid most of the money back to Frank Beechum, I recently bought an additional work truck, and I've also now hired two new employees who run the lawn maintenance crew. This affords me the time now to spend my days recruiting new customers, writing, and attempting to gain exposure for the ASBSF. Just as Burt had predicted, things are moving forward all the time. I've got money coming in, the bills are getting paid, I'm finally getting some respect, and I'm managing to secure a better today for myself and my family, while building toward an even more exciting tomorrow. For the first time in my life I know exactly what I want to do with the rest of it. Thanks to Burt I now have the ability to foresee where it is I am going and how I'm going to get there. I've got a detailed blueprint of how I want my life to play out, and enough moxy left in my bones to make this as close to a reality as I possibly can.

The Package

I happened to have a few weeks straight over the spring where everything seemed to be going my way. Business was booming, we had a good run of beautiful weather (which made landscaping tasks much easier), and I was beginning to make some serious headway with the ASBSF. It was starting to look as if I could do no wrong. And then I got the phone call. It was Dianne (Burt's ex/wife) calling from England, who said that she had been trying to get a hold of me for some time now. I sensed a shake in her voice, and it was becoming clear that this was no social call.

She said that about three weeks back she and Burt had been attempting to tackle some long overdue yard work. She then said that she had gone into the house to fix some fresh lemonade for them both, when, as she returned outside with the beverages, she found Burt slumped onto the ground right next to a large heavy stump that he had been attempting to move by himself. She wasn't seeing any signs of life and was now panic stricken. Dianne quickly looked to see if she could detect any movement in his chest, and it appeared as though he was *not* breathing. She then began to scream for her neighbors to come help as she checked for a pulse, and it was unfortunately to no avail. It was just too late.

Burt had died of a heart failure right there in his backyard. She began to cry now, and blamed herself for not being there. Dianne then apologized to *me*, and I was unsure of what to say. Though I was beginning to feel my knees quake as if my legs were going to suddenly let go, I had quickly realized that I needed to do whatever I must in order to be strong for everyone. This lady was hurting bad and feeling a considerable amount of undeserved guilt. I felt it was up to me to keep it together and help in any way that I could. I asked Dianne if she thought I should try to make my way over there (to the UK) as soon as possible, and she said that she would be OK.

Reminding me of Burt's ability to make friends wherever he would go, she said that there were numerous folks from the area who had offered up their assistance. Also, this having happened three weeks prior, the funeral had of course already taken place. Although I felt terrible that I had missed it, I then remembered how my life as of lately had seemed to be guided somehow. As if a guardian angel had been watching over things and twisting fate to go my way.

Burt was a powerfully influential individual. There is no question that he has changed many lives for the better, and the world will now be forever altered for his having been a part of it. Had he not intervened in *my* life, I can't say for sure where I would be right now. I had only recently found out that there were other guys before myself whom Burt had worked with, and had gone on to do great things. With a little luck and a lot of effort, perhaps Burt's spirit can continue to help others through the creation of this book. I would encourage all who have been affected in any way by his words and ways, to do what they can to help keep his ideals alive, through our accomplishments and our victories over the struggles we each face. Burt wanted each of you to succeed. Let's all try and make a valiant effort not to let him down.

∞

It was about two weeks after I had gotten the call from Dianne that a package arrived at my home, indicating on the return label that it was shipped from London. I was on the road at the time that it had been delivered, but my younger brother called me right away and let me know something had come in. Though it *was* clear where it had come from, I couldn't imagine what on earth it could be. My brother said that it was a box about the size of a briefcase, which had my mind a buzz.

It had been a long hard day, but upon returning home I was reminded of the package, as I had found it leaning against the wall just as I had come in the door. I picked it up, gave it a little shake and it sounded kind of soft'ish. The return label had what I recognized to be Burt's UK address, with Dianne's name. So anyhow, I then proceeded to open the box to find that it was the backpack that I had left at Burt's apartment the night he and I had played ping pong all that time ago. There was also a brief note from Dianne explaining how she knew the bag had belonged to me, thought it looked expensive and realized that I might like to have it back.

Inside the backpack was an old pair of my work boots, which weren't really of any importance. However, there *was* also another item hidden inside a pocket within the main compartment of the bag, one that *was* of a little more interest to me. Tucked within that secret pocket of the backpack was a semi-filled notebook that I could see right away did not belong to me. The cover gave no clue as to its contents, or who's notebook it even was. It was just your everyday college ruled notebook, with nothing written but the words "in" in very small print on the bottom corner of the front cover, and "out" on the back, just above a sequence of characters ($Be_3Al_2SiO_6$) which I had only recently discovered is the chemical formula for emerald (the gem).

As I opened it, I discovered a vast amount of mathematical equations, alchemical writings, random sketches and hand drawn 'charts.' There were also some other writings included that were of rather obscurity and intrigue, although I have yet to determine how one would go about classifying them. It was clear that this was one of Burt's many journals which he had routinely kept, though there wasn't a whole lot of evidence as to what time frame it could have come from. He had just kept so many journals that it was really anyone's guess.

After examining the majority of this notebook's contents, I had come to the realization that there was probably some good useable information held within it. However, I don't know for certain how, or if it is ever going to be possible to make *any* sense out of much of it. I have included one page of the notebook in particular, which I have scanned and provided here so that you may get an idea of the difficulty one might have in finding the true themes behind these various drawings and such. This example was selected for its depiction of the Parazod, as well as the fact that I myself had been able to locate some interesting peculiarities within the image. For instance, within the seven sections of the Parazod figure, are the words: "those/who/find/these/words/in/life, shall/be/thy/brother/through/life's/end." It's not exactly easy to see, but if you look at only the words inside the shape that are not cut off by the lines *of* the shape, read them in a row, then flip the

278

image and repeat the same process, that is what you get.

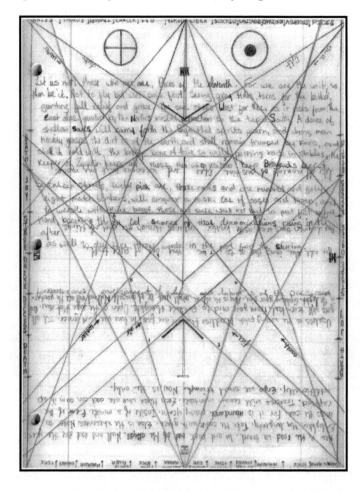

If looked at closely, one can see that this peculiar image has the Parazod figure as the focal point, placed at the very center.

After further examination I had found that there were also some other secrets captured within this image. I was jumbling letters, counting things, pretty much just trying every possible angle that I could think of. One series of characters, I've found, appears to be a date of some kind or some other significant number that I haven't been able to nail down just yet. I have had a few of Burt's other friends take a look at this as well and have yet to learn much of anything new as a result. Still, it *has* been interesting to hear other peoples thoughts on just what it is that 'this or that' could possibly mean.

Though things have been very busy for me, I *have* made an effort to keep close contact with the gentlemen whom Burt had introduced me to, however, this has shown to be increasingly difficult as time wears on. From what I understand, Frank Beechum has taken a position as VP at some other branch of the same corporation. Fortunately, I had managed to pay him back the balance of the money that I owed him *before* this happened, as I'm told the job was located in China. This would also explain why I've yet to ever see him again. Larry the Clown has all but disappeared (as far as *I* know). The meeting I had been to with Mr. Beechum and the other gentlemen was actually the last time I had seen or heard from *him* ever again. And the doctor, *Rosenberg*. Well, I hardly even knew *him* at all. So after a few awkward phone calls between us, I kind of got the feeling that he preferred to stick with his own kind (wealthy). Still yet, he was very cordial nonetheless.

In fact, the one acquaintance that I had made through Burt which *has* turned into a lasting friendship, was with Poseidon, the goldfish which Burt had left behind when he first returned to the UK. Poseidon has been through a lot, and yet he still powers on. As long as he keeps waking up "fins up," he'll be OK.

I had also heard that Dianne was actually doing quite a bit better as of lately, but that she still had a rough road ahead of her. I thought it best to give her some peace and quiet, and I wish her to be well again.

This was the way in which things had played out for me. Though I haven't been able to find the reasoning behind *everything* that had occurred between Burt and I, more and more pieces to this puzzle continue to fall into place as time goes by. Some little mysteries have seemed to remain as such, and some I am just now beginning to understand. And yet there are other pieces to this story which will be revealed in the follow up text, as these are pertinent to the lessons needed further along in this process. I continue to unlock the logic behind the information held within the notebook, and have already made some additional interesting discoveries (to be discussed in sections six and seven).

I have attempted to assist in revealing to those who needed it, their own spark of introspection and motivation within themselves. It is time for all of us to rise above this chaos. To buck this system of addiction and declare that we will no longer allow ourselves to be misguided, misinformed, or misunderstood. I want each of you out there to understand that there is someone rooting for you right here, right this very minute. Grab a fierce grip on that renewed sense of purpose and put it to good use. Get involved in helping others, or contact me and help to bring the country's attention to our needs and to the potential of the ASBSF. Perhaps create your own chapter in your own local area. Maybe you have an exceptional knowledge of natural remedies and would be interested in working toward a solution to the problems surrounding the need for quality, affordable supplements. If this is so, then please let us know. Whether it is here or out there in the world, find a passion and stick with it.

If you have found that you have benefited in some way, or want to get involved in any way, then be sure to visit the website and take part. Also, stay tuned for the follow up text (sections six and seven) due to launch soon.

∞ ∞

Section Five Wrap Up

The individual should now be discovering who they truly are deep down. This last section is primarily about treating every last waking minute available as an opportunity to tweak your life for the better. Yet it also focuses on an individuals commitment to helping others. If you want the world and more, it is going to take a world of effort. But think about the beauty of one day being able to surprise someone, and completely catch them off guard when you tell them that you were at one time an actual heroin addict and your life was all but over. You will be able dazzle others (who will have only known the new you) with stories about how this clean cut successful citizen had once lost it all. The joy that it will bring you to be able to say that you have managed to put all of this behind you, is limitless. Do what is best for you and your family and I assure you that the results will not disappoint. Follow the suggestions laid out here to the best of your ability, and stay tuned for the follow up. I believe there is the potential here to change countless lives, and make history as a result. So get into action and be part of it!

Made in the USA
Middletown, DE
24 June 2018